John Hennig's Exile in Ireland

Gisela Holfter and Hermann Rasche
EDITORS

ARLEN
HOUSE

First published by Arlen House in June 2004

Arlen House
PO Box 222
Galway
Ireland
arlenhouse@ireland.com

ISBN 1-903631-38-6 paperback

Typesetting: Arlen House
Printed by: ColourBooks, Baldoyle, Dublin 13

CONTENTS

ACKNOWLEDGEMENTS

Our thanks are due first and foremost to Monica and Dian Schefold. Without their support and interest in all our research on the life and works of John Hennig, this project would never have been possible. Once again we wish to thank Wolfgang Hennig, Stolberg; Erica Becker, Australia; Prof Angelus Häußling OSB, Maria Laach; Prof Hans Reiss, Bristol; and on the Irish side particularly Dr. Peter Harbison (who launched our *Exil in Irland* book in the Royal Irish Academy), Prof John Harbison, Mrs Sheila Harbison, Noel and Thelma Sheehan, Ann Gallagher, Paula O'Kelly, Kitty O'Sullivan, Sister Ines and Sister Assumpta, Desmond Fennell, Fr. Patrick Twohig, the former Belvedere students John Hyland, Des Reynolds, Sean Schütte and Charlie O'Connor, Victor Laing (Military Archives), Miriam Tiernan (Department of Foreign Affairs), Elisabeth O'Neill and Katherine Meenan (Bord na Mona).

We would like to thank Eoin Bourke, Paul Dowling, Jean Conacher, Clive Earls, Siobhan O'Connor, Claire Ryan, Mark Stansbury and especially Glenn Cooper and Susan Tebbutt for their assistance. The autobiography was translated principally by Cathy Rappolt, and given to us by Monica Schefold.

The Irish Research Council for Humanities and Social Sciences (IRCHSS) has given us invaluable help to the whole project "German-speaking exiles in Ireland 1933-1945" through a research grant. The support of the College of Humanities Research Funding at the University of Limerick was also very important. We are grateful to both the University of Limerick and the National University of Ireland, Galway and our splendid colleagues there. And last but not least we sincerely thank Alan Hayes of Arlen House publishers, for his support.

FOREWORD

After the death of my father John Hennig in 1986 we found his manuscript *Die bleibende Statt*. The title is taken from the Bible (Hebrew 13, 14). The manuscript was written in German and was found amongst quite a few other unpublished articles and materials. We decided to get the manuscript, which was quite complete and ready for publication, printed privately as a book, despite the fact that my father had probably written it more for himself than with the thought of having it published.

The text describes his early life on the continent, his studies at various German universities and then the years in Ireland in exile. It was written after his return to the continent, to Basle (Switzerland) in 1956, and appears to me to have been a text which, despite his uprootedness and the contrasting elements, brings his life into a certain unity.

Part of this unity are the years in Ireland, and the book contains many memories, reflections and details of that period of now more than half a century ago. In fact his thoughts went back more and more to the Irish experience in the last years of his life.

It is therefore a source of great happiness for the family that, almost twenty years after John Hennig's death, the translated publication of the chapters concerning Ireland has been made possible by the exceptional interest and engagement of Dr. Gisela Holfter and Dr. Hermann Rasche. It is to their great merit that they have been gathering up the traces of my father's life and work and published the book *Exil in Irland* in 2002 with an introduction, the two Ireland-related chapters of *Die bleibende Statt* and many of his publications on German-Irish relations.

Composing that book they have brought to light the outer circumstances surrounding the chapters on John Hennig's life in Ireland, on how he worked and on what subjects. It seems to me that they almost know more about my father than we ourselves do, through their thorough and conscientious research, thus making his life and work more easily accessible to the English speaking world. For this we are most grateful.

Monica Schefold
Bremen, 20 May 2004

PREFACE

Many people have asked us for an English version of the introduction to the life and work of John Hennig, which we wrote for *Exil in Irland: John Hennigs Schriften zu deutsch-irischen Beziehungen* (WVT Wissenschaftlicher Verlag Trier, Germany, 2002). In that book we brought together John Hennig's most important articles dealing with German-Irish relations. These articles had originally been published in over thirty different academic journals, newspapers and other publications and had not been easily accessible. Hennig wrote many of his articles in English and they were presented in that book.

For this second publication we have translated our extensive introduction to his life and work, together with a translation of the two chapters from his privately published autobiography *Die bleibende Statt* (*The Lasting Abode*) that deal with Ireland.

Gisela Holfter and Herman Rasche
Limerick and Galway,
May 2004

John Hennig: His Life and Work

John Hennig,
who to all intents and purposes
created the field of Irish-German literary relations

- P. O'Neill, *Ireland and Germany*, 1985

This is the story of a remarkable person. After Nazi policies forced him and his family into exile in 1939, John[1] Hennig found refuge in Ireland. From that period onwards the complex relationship between his new homeland and his country of birth became one of his main areas of research. Hennig showed his great interest in and aptitude for academic work not only through teaching and research, but primarily through the publication of hundreds of papers, most notably in history, literature and liturgy. Yet throughout his whole life he was able to pursue his academic work only as a secondary occupation. As Hennig's sister Erica remembers, he remarked that:

> he didn't actually know why he wrote so much, since so few people would be interested in it [...] and he would soon be forgotten along with his research.[2]

That, however, has fortunately not been the case: there are various collections of his essays,[3] and he is highly respected in the area of Irish-German Studies.[4] Nevertheless, despite this limited acclaim, his research is only visible in references in a few key articles, most of his essays are extremely difficult to obtain and the number and diversity of his publications are known to only a few specialists. Even his name is often unfamiliar to those interested in German-Irish themes. There are various reasons for this, such as the fact that his publications appeared in so many different places and that he worked freelance, without the support of an academic institution.

What is equally striking is the range of themes in Hennig's writing. A reader of his academic works would hardly suspect that he also composed tracts with tips for coping with illness on the one hand or an imminent wedding on the other ('... don't forget to brush your eyebrows and lashes as a very last contribution to perfect grooming' from *The Bride's Book*, Dublin, 1941). In his privately published autobiography *Die bleibende Statt*,[5] Hennig himself speaks doubtfully of his remarkably versatile part-time work as a writer. (*Autobiography*, 11).

Hennig was born in Leipzig on 3 March 1911, the fourth child of Max Hennig (born 10 December 1871 in Meißen on the Elbe) and Johanna Clemen (born 12 June 1877 in Grimma on the Mulde). He was baptised Paul Gottfried Johannes and was usually called Hans. At the time of his birth, his family lived in Funkenburgstraße and in October 1912 moved to Auenstraße 2. Prior to embarking on a teaching career, Max Hennig had received a Ph.D. for his study on A.E. Biedermann's *Psychology of Religious Perception*; he taught religion and Hebrew at König-Albert-Gymnasium in Leipzig. John Hennig's mother, whom Max had met through fellow student Otto Clemen, had been a deaconess and had a preference for pious church services; family life was characterised by great devoutness, books and frugality.[6]

John Hennig was a child at the time of the First World War and was a pupil at the famous Thomas School [Thomasschule], where he was a member of the day-boys' school choir. An enormous capacity for work, academic talent, and diligence were among his outstanding characteristics. In his recollections, Ernst, John Hennig's older brother by six years, noted that:

> the very gifted 'little brother' skipped the last primary
> school class and, in contrast to his brothers, completed the

prescribed curriculum as far as the *Abitur* [Leaving Certificate] in just 12 years.[7]

His younger sister Erica agreed that he was:

> by far the cleverest of us five children, in everything that he did and said, [was] mature and confident, extremely independent and a clear thinker, already critically analytical as a young person.[8]

But Hennig was aware that as a young boy he often was unable to relate to his peers. He felt isolated in the Youth Movement (*Autobiography*, 53). In school he was painfully aware of this isolation. But he did not see himself as the 'eccentric recluse' that his classmates thought him to be (*Autobiography*, 58). In a letter to his oldest brother, Karl, in 1981, he writes: 'I was also politically isolated, because [...] I had been a radical pacifist since 1924 (Jamboree in Copenhagen)'.[9] After disassociating himself mentally from the Youth Movement, which he had joined because of his older brothers, he began to spend his free time doing solo bicycle tours. His first big trip at the age of fifteen took him through 'Saxon Switzerland' to Bohemia. The following year he cycled through Northern Bavaria and the Rhineland.[10] On Sundays he went cycling in order to relax after the exhausting week. When he was fourteen, Hennig began giving two to four hours of daily private grinds to younger students. He later remembers that at sixteen he was allowed into the German Library where he often read until ten in the evening, and only then began his homework (*Autobiography*, 56). One can still sense Hennig's joy when after having passed his *Abitur* he was able to spend all his time in this learned institution. There he first read Jaspers's *Philosophie* and Joyce's *Ulysses* — two works that, for very different reasons, were later to play a crucial role in his life (*Autobiography*, 64).

Student Days

Hennig spent the winter and summer semesters of 1929–30 in Bonn, his first alma mater. He studied modern languages (German, English and French), but his main interest was philosophy. His uncle, Paul Clemen, a much respected professor of art history at the university, and his family offered Hennig accommodation 'in the house wonderfully situated by the Rhine' (*Autobiography*, 70). And through his relatives he got to know many prominent people from the world of art, science and business (in fact, during his studies in Bonn, Berlin and Leipzig he encountered numerous stars of the German academic world).[11] Even though Hennig recalled that during his studies in Bonn he frequently felt 'dejected' (*Autobiography*, 70), he also experienced numerous positive features of university life. During his time in Bonn he met Kläre Meyer, who was studying art history there and knew Paul Clemen through a relative. Shortly before his seventieth birthday Hennig wrote to his brother Karl[12] about the 'fateful encounter': 'The most decisive turning point in my life was of course my meeting Claire [...] as Adalbert Stifter would say: pure providence'.[13] When he met Claire, Hennig was just about to turn nineteen and Claire was four years older. Their family backgrounds were very different: Claire (as she was called from their time in Dublin onwards), was from a well-to-do Jewish family and led a life free of financial worries thanks to income from the roughly 250 patents and technical innovations created by her father, Felix Meyer.[14] Despite these differences it became clear to Hennig even after a few months that he had found his partner for life and he wrote home accordingly. He had already told Claire at their first dance that he wanted to marry her. She did not take him seriously and replied: 'Are you totally crazy?' (*Autobiography*, 95).

But after knowing each other for just one semester, Hennig went to Berlin, where he enrolled in theological studies, which would enable him to opt later to enter the protestant church. His relationship with Claire during this time was maintained by sporadic visits and above all through countless letters.

During his time at Berlin University (three years before the Nazis seized power), when it was almost taken for granted that students became radical, Hennig did not join any group. He replied indignantly to attempts to recruit him: 'Leave me alone, I am an individualist'. (*Autobiography*, 75).

After studying in Berlin, Hennig returned to Leipzig in the winter semester of 1930–31 to continue his studies there. By then he knew for definite that he wanted to pursue an academic career. The premature death of his father after an unsuccessful brain tumour operation in 1931 affected him deeply and he decided that, in addition to obtaining his Ph.D., he would sit the state exams in order to have more job security. In the final days of his eighth semester at university, just a few weeks after the proclamation of the 'Third Reich', he handed in his project for the state exam and presented his Ph.D. thesis on the earliest possible submission date. His dissertation addressed 'The Conception and Categories of Life: Studies on the History and Theory of Concept Formation with special reference to Wilhelm Dilthey'. He had begun this dissertation under the supervision of the religious philosopher Joachim Wach[15] and completed it under the supervision of Theodor Litt.[16] Litt expressed a very favourable view in his assessment of the dissertation, albeit with some critical observations:

> This dissertation, with the scope of the material covered in it and also the significance of the topics dealt with, appears to be close to the level of an inaugural dissertation. However, due to an almost incredible amount of reading done in his eight semesters and his treatment of all periods of philosophy and knowledge — he uncovers parallels, interpretations, further developments — he confronts the reader with far more material and interrelationships than one would expect from such a theme. [...] To that extent the

dissertation appears worthy of the highest praise. However, it cannot be denied that one cannot always be happy with these achievements. It cannot be overlooked that this rooting around in the history of ideas is in some ways not typical of a young person. One would have preferred it if such a gifted young man had concentrated less on gathering so much material and had more courage in deriving his own findings. That is not to say that the researched material is lacking in analysis! The dissertation leaves an ambivalent impression, and it is difficult to come to a just verdict. If one judges the student's performance as a whole and compares it with what is normally produced in other dissertations, then in my opinion, despite my expressed reservations, the candidate should not be denied the mark

I (Very good).

It seems to me impossible to demand a revision of the dissertation. This would present an unbearable strain due to the superabundance of material which has been analysed and assembled with such infinite diligence.

– 25.3.33 Litt[17]

The other examiner, Felix Krueger,[18] took a different view on a number of important points. Although there was initially widespread agreement on the basic assessment of the candidate's abilities,[19] in his judgment of the dissertation, Krueger came to a significantly different conclusion. Krueger disagreed that the 'abundance of knowledge' was striking, given the age and study time of the candidate. Krueger spoke of Hennig's 'weak organisational ability' and narrow 'intellectual capacity' (which actually contradicted his first assessment). Rather cuttingly, he claimed an alleged lack of knowledge about advances in 'psychological and biological research. Stuck behind his many books, mostly secondary literature, he hardly casts a glance at the actual reality'.[20] Though it cannot be proved that National Socialist ideas were already making their mark, one can suspect that Krueger, as a founder of the 'Leipzig

School' of Psychology, certainly expounded narrowly defined opinions in his area of expertise.

Hennig later wrote about possible political reasons for this unfavourable reception, which he was informed about by his brother. Krueger refused to grant a degree which he said was 'inspired by the "half-Jewish [Professor] Wach"' (*Autobiography*, 100). Krueger's criticism of Hennig's dissertation 'arousing in the reader a feeling of being hounded' does not sound totally implausible. One only has to think of the circumstances under which the dissertation was written. A systematic revision of his work was just not possible for Hennig (one should also remember that before computers arrived and made many things much easier, one could not just quickly insert corrections). He was under severe pressure to complete the state exams at the same time and in addition, political developments were directly affecting his personal life. In *Die bleibende Statt* Hennig describes how the dissertation was produced. He finally ended up dictating it to a typist. One day, the woman who was doing his typing said: 'Do you see the woman over there? She has a Jewish sweetheart'. Two days later she reported that the woman and her sweetheart had been arrested (*Autobiography*, 97). This extra pressure on Hennig, whose thoughts of course turned to his Jewish fiancée, must have been enormous. It must have been clear to him that if he married Claire, he would have no chance of an academic career (he was already aware in 1932 that a career in the service of the Protestant church was highly unlikely with a Jewish wife (*Autobiography*, 97)). Shortly after seeing a photo in the paper, which showed a man carrying a sign saying: 'I had sex with a Jewish bitch', he wrote to Claire that it was now time for them to marry. On 10 April 1933, in the middle of his preparations for the oral state exams he travelled on the night train to Aachen, married Claire the following morning in a registry office and travelled back alone on the night train to Leipzig (*Autobiography*, 97f).

It is not known how much Krueger knew of the planned wedding.[21] On 13 April 1933 he proposed that the work be given back for revision. For his part, Litt proposed that the work be given a Grade II and the dissertation would consequently be presented to the Faculty of Philosophy for approval. The subsequent positions of the other professors in the faculty are recorded in the archives and make interesting reading. The support for Krueger's assertion that the work should be handed back sound just as interesting as the arguments in favour of accepting it. For example: 'After much thought and scrutiny of the work, I must agree totally with the verdict and recommendations of Messrs Krueger, Volkelt and Junker' on the basis of the student's 'indulgences in muddled trains of thought, though I know him personally as an excellent young man'. Some of those in favour also sound ambivalent:

> The candidate is fairly well known to me as a participant in my classes and from personal interaction. The objections brought forward against his work concur with my impression of his personality […] For this reason, however, I can't agree with 'returning for revision', because no revision can correct the faults, which are clearly more than superficial in nature. The candidate would have to contradict himself if he was to totally satisfy the expressed criteria for changes […] For this reason the work must be decided upon in its current form: acceptance or rejection? Since the unquestionably high academic quality of the candidate and commendable quality of his work make a rejection of the work impossible in my view, I agree therefore with the stance of Mr. Litt.[22]

But the abstentions were most frequent ('Because I am having difficulty in making a judgement on the dissertation, even after intense scrutiny, I abstain from voting'). The result was 12 votes for acceptance with a Grade II, 6 votes for handing back the work for revision and 26 professors abstained. The oral exam took place afterwards on 20 July 1933 and was, as Hennig recalls, 'a farce' (*Autobiography*, 100). From the historian Helmut Berve he received a 'good' for ancient history (his knowledge of the Augustinian period does not appear to have been so outstanding), whilst Litt in his assessment ('Very good') reiterated that the oral examination also '*thoroughly* reaffirms' (emphasis in original) his favourable assessment of the dissertation. In his German course with Georg Witkowski, the Ph.D. supervisor of the writer Erich Kästner, he ended up with 'very good' (Hennig's recollections of this particular exam, the last one for Witkowski, who was later dismissed for political reasons, can be found in *Die bleibende Statt*).[23]

Since there was no prospect of pursuing an academic career, Hennig was obliged to start looking for a job. His father-in-law offered him the chance of working in his firm in Aachen. Claire's family 'kindly but reluctantly' took Hennig in. Claire's father had wished for Jewish men for his daughters, 'because he was firmly convinced that only with Jewish men could a woman be certain not to be beaten' (*Autobiography*, 96). He had also taken a critical view of Hennig's studies, which he regarded with 'thinly disguised disdain' (*Autobiography*, 98). The Hennig family appears to have taken Claire into their midst without any problems – 'Claire soon became the darling of all of us. Her precious personality: warm, generous, very understanding, loving. We adored her …'.[24] Mrs. Hennig's letters from the 1930s also sound very warm and show a great deal of affection, e.g. when she writes to Claire ('my Klärchen'):

> I can vividly imagine your description of Hans's amazement when he discovered the wonderful library in the Jesuit seminary. If I were you, I would have been worried about whether he would ever bring himself to leave there![25]

His father, who as his brother Ernst remembers, was greatly interested in Jewish spirituality, had also been very interested in other religions and in philosophical questions.[26]

Working Life in Aachen

Hennig's new work environment, the firm German Rotawerke Ltd., specialised in the manufacture of precision machinery and produced many of Felix Meyer's patented products. It was founded in 1909 and in 1937 became known as 'Rota Equipment and Machine Manufacture Felix Meyer KG'. Felix Meyer, Claire's father, was very highly regarded and was seen as a creative inventor and salesman. He came from a Jewish family which could be traced back to the 16th century in Westphalia, and had been based in Aachen since the early nineteenth century. He grew up in a liberal Jewish household, embedded in the 'tradition of classical German culture' (*Autobiography*, 98). Even as the anti-Jewish laws became more severe right up until 'Reichskristallnacht' in 1938, he did not want to believe that anything bad could happen to him. He reacted morosely to Hennig's suggestion to emigrate.[27] It was clear to Hennig that in accepting the offer to work in his father-in-law's company he would face hard years 'unprepared, dependent and hopeless' (*Autobiography*, 98). The contrast between his previous life and background and his new life in his parents-in-law's imposing house was considerable. In 1935 the young couple moved into the castle-like property 'Bodenhof'[28] opposite his in-laws' house. Both their first two daughters, Gabriele and Monica, were born there, in 1936 and 1938 respectively. The Hennigs had two housemaids and a chauffeur employed by the firm. (*Autobiography*, 106). This well-to-do and apparently worry-free situation, albeit involving Hennig in a high level of dependency on Claire's father, stood in sharp contrast to the encroaching and accelerating political pressure. In spring 1938 Claire had to hand over her shares in the company to her non-Jewish husband; in July 1938 Felix Meyer withdrew as an unlimited partner in the company and Hennig, together with a long-serving employee, replaced him as unlimited partners. The National Socialist authorities demanded that one of their affiliated personnel be taken on in the company in line with 'Aryanisation'. On 10 November Felix Meyer was temporarily arrested. He was forbidden from entering the premises, on whose entrance the employees had already painted a large swastika. At the beginning of February 1939, he was permitted to emigrate to Belgium, from where his wife originated. They settled in Le Zoute. The condition for this was that Hennig and his family had to vouch for the fact that Felix Meyer would not establish a rival firm abroad. On 6 February the words 'Felix Meyer' in the company title were replaced with 'Dr. Hennig'.[29]

During that period, Hennig managed to pursue his research interests, as well as working at his job and caring for a growing family. In 1936 he published a response to Karl Jaspers'[30] *Vernunft und Existenz*.[31] Having sent Jaspers the article he received an invitation to visit, and then drove from a trade fair in Frankfurt to Heidelberg for the meeting. An immediate rapport grew between them. Their friendship led to private visits; because of the Jewish descent of Gertrud Jaspers, the Jaspers could not go away on holiday, so they spent a few days with the Hennigs at Bodenhof in the summer of 1939.[32] Hennig explains in his autobiography that no man, apart from his father and brother Karl, had as large an influence on his life as Jaspers (*Autobiography*, 116). Hennig had a further life-defining contact with another former pupil of the Leipzig Thomas School, Heinrich Keller, the Rector of the Jesuit College in Valkenburg in Holland (1894–1942). In 1936 Hennig made the decision to convert to Catholicism. With the birth of their second daughter (Monica), Claire also decided to become a Catholic. Hennig's conversion had not been easy for Claire: 'As she was about to sign the paper whereby we promised to raise our children as Catholics, she burst into tears' (*Autobiography*, 111f). Their different cultural heritages remained important and were a source of pride for both of them.

Establishing Contact with Ireland

Their first contact with Ireland came about through Heinrich Keller. At this point in time it was clear that they would have to emigrate. Ireland was seen as a possible destination. Keller introduced him to an Irish Jesuit, who had a short discussion with Hennig, declared his English adequate to teach German there, and said he would speak on Hennig's behalf about a job. A few days later, a card from the Rector of Belvedere College, a boys' school in Dublin run by the Jesuits, was posted on to Hennig from Valkenburg: 'If you can teach a few hours German for us, we will pay you thirty shillings per week' (*Autobiography*, 117). Hennig secured a visa from the British Consulate in Cologne for a fact-finding trip to Ireland and he visited Dublin in Easter 1939. His first impressions were not altogether positive:

> Of course it was raining in Dublin. Everything was clammy and, I thought, dirty. The Rector showed me the school. The highlight was the laboratory where there was a proper set of scales, a rack with dusty test tubes and a few boxes with exotic plants. At the Department of External Affairs, I received a questionnaire with instructions to fill it in, send it to the relevant Irish mission in Paris and there it would be checked and sent back to Dublin. I would then hear from them. (*Autobiography*, 117f)

The Department had indicated that there could be a period of a few months before Hennig would receive an answer, and this was, in light of an ever more probable outbreak of war, understandably very stressful for Hennig. Furthermore, Ireland was not recommended as a country to emigrate to. Hennig had met a clergyman to whom he had confided that he intended to emigrate to Ireland:

> Are you crazy? […] People there have a bottle of whiskey in
> their right pocket, a rosary in their left pocket, and a
> revolver in their back pocket (*Autobiography*, 117).

At the end of August the situation deteriorated to the point that
Claire decided to flee to Belgium. On 26 August 1939, a few
days before war broke out, Hennig left Aachen and went to
Belgium legally, because as he said: 'I still believed in the law'
(*Autobiography*, 118). During the oppressive wait for the long-
term residence permit for Ireland, Hennig moved into his
brother Karl's house who was the pastor in Eupen (Belgium).
Hennig intended to return to Germany as soon as he was
ordered back to present for military duty. The morning after
this summons arrived, came the news that his visa had arrived
in Paris (cf. translation of the two Ireland chapters from *Die
bleibende Statt* in this edition).

The granting of this visa was the result of an intensive and
detailed correspondence between different Ministries and the
Refugee Committee, which is further evidence of the difficulties
and bureaucratic hurdles facing German refugees; but Hennig,
probably to his good fortune, did not know about this
correspondence.

In the summer of 1939, the 'Irish Co-ordinating Committee
for Refugees' moved a resolution to secure a residence permit
for Hennig, signed by its secretary Colum Gavan Duffy. On the
basis of this a notification followed on 31 July from the
Department of Justice to the Department of External Affairs
that such a motion had been proposed. The letter explains:

> The Irish Co-ordinating Committee have satisfied the
> Minister that Johannes Hennig is a suitable person for
> admission and I am accordingly to request you to authorize
> the Legation at Berlin to grant a visa to Johannes Hennig.
> The Department of Industry and Commerce are granting a
> permit for the employment of Dr. Hennig in Belvedere
> College during his temporary residence in this country. The

permit will be sent to the Department of External Affairs and I am to suggest that you forward it to the Legation in Berlin when informing the Legation of the authorisation for the granting of the visa.[33]

In the letter 'Berlin' was subsequently underlined and the handwritten comment 'Paris?' was added in the margin. The Irish authorities also realized that a visit by Hennig to Berlin would probably not have been advisable. Hennig wrote again to the 'Irish Legation' in Paris asking whether the visa could be issued in or sent to Belgium and he could pick it up in Brussels. In addition he required a transit visa for Great Britain that would only be guaranteed by British representatives in Brussels once the Irish had stamped a residence permit in his passport. John was issued with a visa. For Claire however, who was still in Belgium, the uncertainty increased. War had meanwhile broken out and there was imminent danger that Belgium would be occupied by German troops. Hennig was registered under the number G.S. 14548, with the note 'permitted to land in Ireland on condition that he remains therein not later than 8. Aug. 1940'.[34]

Ireland

Hennig's diary entry on 6 October 1939 describes the crossing and his first impressions of Ireland – written in English, interestingly:

I got a splendid berth, Schrödinger travelled 1st class. On deck people were first singing and blowing bagpipe [sic], then they all felt seasick [...] appointment with Fr. Rector. Studienleiter. Seen the schoolhouse. I have agreed to teach interesting and objective political opinions. Letters. Supper (eggs).[35]

These weeks must have been very difficult not only for Claire, who was still waiting in Belgium for a visa, but also for Hennig, who was alone in a foreign country and had to sort out lodgings and a job and did not know when or if his wife and children would make it out of Belgium. Ireland was certainly not a country that willingly accepted those seeking refuge; on the contrary, only a very limited number were let into the country, and then only under tight bureaucratic restrictions.[36]

A letter from John to Claire, dated four days after his arrival in Ireland and written partly in German and partly in English, gives an insight into his situation at that time, his obvious loneliness, the political uncertainty and also his perception of the main cultural differences:

> Darling,
>
> I hope my letter of this afternoon telling that your visa will be granted this week reaches you in due course. I shall try to get the official statement or the certificate of the committee as quickly as possible.
>
> By the way, I hear that Ireland has admitted till now in the whole 110 (hundred and ten) immigrants from Central Europe of which 40 are Catholics (I know already 5 of them!). So it seems that the danger, had [illegible] to be kicked out is not urgent.
>
> I do not understand the consequences of the last political events. In any case, it seems the best we come here. What people is fearing is that if the war will be more vehement over England, thousands and thousands of Irish refugees will come back to Eire and increase the unemployment. [...]
>
> [The following part was originally in German]
>
> I gained a somewhat better impression of the life and possibilities here than the last time. There are very beautiful doors in the city.
>
> I am so longing for some word from you! Of course, you'll send me a telegram if there is something wrong, but I can't do anything from here. The way back is as closed off as anything could be. Dearest, I have the feeling that it is a

good life that awaits you here, though not easy. [*English again from here*] I am deeply prepared to do my ever best in all times.

The boy-teachers whose acquaintance I made today make the impression 2–3. Mr. Gavan Duffy is a splendid man of one of the best families. I am on best speaking terms with him and he will help me a lot. I make the experience Vati made too: We have quite another tempo of living as this people. The end of the week is for them what for us is the next hour.

All my love to you all. Kiss the chicken. Her photograph decided the official to give the visa. Thousand kisses

Hans

[*written afterwards in the margin*]

[...) Can you send me the type writing paper at least 300 pages (no carbon copy!). It is so expensive here.

This is my fourth letter from Eire. It contains 2 pages and one annex and is posted Monday night.[37]

Hennig's powerlessness and his total reliance on the good will of others is highlighted by the anecdotal reference to the securing of visas, showing the arbitrariness of some official decisions. There was some help both from the previously mentioned Gavan Duffy and the Refugee Committee, and from the Austrian physicist and Nobel Prize winner Erwin Schrödinger, whom he had met on the crossing to Ireland as they were both going into exile.[38] Schrödinger is also mentioned in the diary in the days which followed and there were telephone calls and invitations to dinner for the young German companion. While his first concern was for his family, he also had to cope not only with the new unfamiliar surroundings but also with a new career.

'Twenty-four hours after my arrival in this country I stood before a class of boys and started teaching'.[39] The teaching contract with Belvedere College, whose illustrious past pupils famously once included James Joyce, was – just like his

26

residence permit – limited initially to one year. Giving German lessons was relatively problem-free since Ireland had successfully maintained its neutrality and there was no marked antipathy towards Germany. In the early days of the war support for Germany in the fight against England was widespread and not confined to nationalist circles.[40]

The contact between students and teachers in Belvedere College often seems to have been quite cordial.[41] Indeed, in *Die bleibende Statt* one can read of Hennig's exhortation that the students should not work too hard. Hennig's classes seemed to have reacted sympathetically to what he himself called his 'imperfect English' and resisted giggling at it. One of his students, the Irish author Desmond Fennell, who took German classes in 1945–46, remembers Hennig as a very good teacher, the only one who ever invited him back to his house (Fennell got a distinction for his knowledge of German and afterwards studied in Dublin and Bonn).[42] Hennig followed the contents of the prescribed schoolbooks and spoke very little of Germany; he spoke above all about literature. Other students of Belvedere College still remember the young teacher who was conspicuous because of his intensity and his dress ('you noticed him in a crowd') and who during his first months of teaching also seemed, not surprisingly, somewhat nervous. The students' recollections of Hennig are generally very positive.[43]

The language used by the family – at least in the later years in Ireland – was English. Hennig writes in *Die Bleibende Statt*: 'The mother tongue in our family was the language that the grandparents painstakingly tried to learn from their grand-children' (*Autobiography*, 175).

At the beginning of their time in Ireland, it seems that Claire at least found it important to speak German with the children, which led to the two-year-old daughter Monica speaking a 'brilliant double Dutch'.[44] The question remains how Hennig managed within a few months after his arrival, to write his articles in English. He already had fairly good English before coming to Ireland, as a young child he had contact with the English language through relations and his parents' acquaintances and he had also learned English at school.[45] While studying, particularly in Bonn, he attended further English classes as documented by his academic certificates. The first entries in his diary, which begin with his crossing to Ireland, are written in English. Later on one can also find entries in German. One can assume that, in addition to the usual corrections made by the journal editors, Irish colleagues or acquaintances helped him with proof-reading his articles. An interesting piece of information is contained in a memo, in which Hennig is informed of a potential student who does not have enough money to pay for classes, but offers to proof-read Hennig's English articles in return for receiving German lessons.[46]

The following extract from a letter to his mother-in-law Marguerite Meyer on 5 May 1940 provides an insight into Hennig's work environment 6 months after arriving in Ireland:

> You inquire about my work. I have a few more private students. It's now hardly possible to get any students, firstly, because of the time of year, secondly, because of the excessive supply of emigrants who are offering a cheaper service. I hope to get a few more students in the college in the New Year. I am also teaching French and would like to teach Latin. 2½ month's holidays are coming soon; the college will pay me during them.[47] I am writing a German schoolbook specifically for Irish students, with reference to their school situation, to Ireland and above all to Irish, which I am learning. It is very interesting because it has kept its ancient features, which have been lost in all other languages and it has, as a Celtic language, a special character. There are many interesting points of comparison with German, which have not yet been fully evaluated.
>
> Since I have been here, I have had a large project in mind, which is taking up a lot of time: an investigation of Latin as

spoken by the Church. This project has various aspects, not only linguistic but also philosophical and of course theological, cultural and historical. It is a topic that certainly needs further exploration. Of course one would need the undisturbed and quiet life of a monk.

Philosophy is a grossly neglected area here, nobody is interested in it, a good preparation in case one should travel to the USA. At the moment, however, throughout the whole world spiritual life and especially philosophical thought are of course in short supply.[48]

From September 1940, in Hennig's correspondence one can increasingly see his thoughts about emigrating to the USA out of fear of an invasion, as already indicated in his letter to Marguerite. The conditions included securing a sworn affidavit and a guarantee from a US citizen, which was problematic.[49] In February 1941 John Hennig saw an even greater difficulty in securing a passage to America.[50] The situation was especially tragic in light of the fact that, in 1938, emigration to the USA would have been possible after Felix and Marguerite Meyer's visit there and was something that was very much favoured by John Hennig, who saw opportunities in the USA. However, Felix Meyer refused the idea point-blank[51] and recalled this with a bad conscience in a letter to Ireland in 1941:

Your stupid dad sends his kisses and hugs. He is to blame for your unhappiness because of his German patriotism. When I tell people here that I was in America with mum in '38 and could have lived very happily there, but that I returned to Germany because of homesickness, people tell me that I don't deserve to be doing so well because I was such an idiot and perhaps they are right.[52]

In May 1940 the family decided to move from Clontarf, where they had been living since November 1939, because the situation with their landlord became untenable (after arriving in Ireland, Hennig had stayed the first few weeks in the

Belvedere Hotel, Great Denmark Street). He wrote to his brother Karl about this on a card and also told of his private and his 'real' life, i.e. his research:

> [...] It is a pity that we have to leave this flat as our landlord behaved impossibly towards us. We hope we find a place by the sea, but it is hard as this is the most expensive season. Weather is lovely, we had again marvellous impressions from the scenery round Dublin. My work is rather delayed as I have to do some housework. Thanks ever so much for the Lesebuch, which will be of tremendous help to me. Could you send me once a small Luther-bible? Thanks too for the K.d.U. it is the first time I really understand Kant. This work appeared 150 years ago and I think it is the first 'philosophical anthropology'. In spite of these times I remain a philosopher, but it is hard to see no outlook. Claire and the children are all right, but Claire needs badly a recovery time. Let me have all news about mother and the geschwister. Give my love to Trudel and the kids. With all our love, Hans[53] [*written in English in the original*]

Claire was not very well at this time. The first spring in Ireland brought with it sickness which is described in *Die bleibende Statt*. Both the children and Claire were suffering from whooping cough and the eldest daughter Gabriele developed a life-threatening lung complication.

After these difficulties were overcome and the Hennigs almost miraculously found far more suitable accommodation in the Burrow Road in Sutton, life in Ireland began to get better. A house and garden offered the children a lot of space to run around, and directly behind the garden lay a wonderful beach around Dublin Bay. A housemaid provided some relief for Claire, who was not yet fully recovered from illness. This probably gave the impression of a certain amount of affluence to the neighbours.[54] The Hennigs were able to hire the maid due to the sporadic payments from the English firm Jorgensen &

Johnson to John Hennig for the use of the patents of Felix Meyer. However, Hennig saw this as borrowed money and desperately tried not to touch the money at all but to provide for his family by his own means.[55]

Increasing social contacts helped the Hennig family to settle in; in his autobiography Hennig mentions the medieval historian Ludwig Bieler[56] as one of the few who encouraged him in his activity as an author (*Autobiography*, 143). There was also contact with other exiles such as the bacteriologist Hans Sachs and his wife Lotte[57] who became good friends also with Claire and acted as kind of surrogate grandparents for the children. They visited each other regularly:

> Claire and I are on very good terms with Prof. and Mrs. Sachs, a famous physiologist from Heidelberg, a friend of our friend Jaspers, we see them at least twice a week. Prof. Sachs is very musical and every Monday they have a little concert in their house, attended by Prof. Sachs and Dr. Bieler, another friend of ours, a palaeographer from Vienna, who sings very nicely. Often he sings Schubert songs. He and his wife as well as a young doctor, born in Neuss, and his wife come often to us.[58] [*written in English in the original*]

Hennig, whom his brother Ernst regarded as the most musical of the five children,[59] played the violin as a child and, while in Ireland, seems to have managed to play from time to time.[60] The settling-in process went well in other ways, too. An opportunity even presented itself for Hennig to get to know his adopted country better. In a letter to his sister-in-law Margot Junod about the move to Sutton, he enthused about his first large-scale discovery of Ireland, a trip to Connemara for a few days:

> I was taken for the caravan-trip by the brother of one of my pupils, who is now one of our best friends. We were five in the caravan, all belonging to the Oxford-Group, of which you will perhaps have heard as it is rather strong in your country. I had the most marvellous impressions not only of

these companions but also of the scenery and the country folk. We spent a week in Connemara, the outskirts of Europe, w[h]ere people live in the same conditions as thousand years ago, and we had the most brilliant contact with them especially by splendid campfires. I have learnt in these few days more than else in years. The scenery is indescribable, the beauty of Norway combined with that of Italy. I could not imagine a landscape more appealing to me. The combination of mountains, woods and water (sea, lakes, torrents rivers in steep valleys etc.) and the wonderful character of the people is most impressive.[61] [*written in English in the original*]

A Possible Spy Under Surveillance

While Hennig enthused about his trip to the West of Ireland and remembered it for many years afterwards (cf. his depiction in *Die bleibende Statt*), he was scarcely aware that he was under surveillance for the whole duration of the trip. He evidently aroused suspicion after Irish Surveillance (G2 Military Intelligence) received information from a 'friendly German national' at the end of April 1940 that:

> Joannes (sic) Hennig, German [...] was worthy of attention. This information was not elaborated upon by informant. Henning (sic) is ostensibly a refugee. He arrived in the country on 6/10/39. His movements are now being subjected to surveillance.[62]

The following week his name appeared, together with three or four other names of German nationals, on the surveillance list:

> Attention was given to the movements etc. of Johannes Hennig, German National residing in 11, Copeland Ave, Clontarf. Subject was not observed to engage in any suspicious activities. He called to the *Evening Herald* offices on a number of occasions but it is believed the reason for his

visits there is due to the fact that he is seeking (sic) house accommodation through the advertising columns of that paper.[63]

The report 18719 also found it important to mention: 'Not in possession of a car'. It was therefore no wonder that the notification Hennig felt compelled to give to the local police station of his intended absence for two weeks in the West of Ireland caused a flurry of activity. A fellow traveller was contacted in order to keep an eye on Hennig's activities.[64] On 9 September came the clearance statement:

> Re: Supervision of Aliens – Hennig, Johannes, German National, The Burrow, Sutton, Co. Dublin. Reference previous reports on above named, I beg to state that Hennig and party returned from the tour towards the end of July. The Alien did not engage in suspicious activity of any kind during his absence. The question raised in last paragraph of minute of Ard-Cheannphort at Bray was dealt with in report furnished on 12th July, 1940. The delay in returning this file is regretted and was brought about by reason of illness of member of party who accompanied Hennig on the tour and who had promised to supply information if he acted suspiciously.[65]

At times, it was even believed that Hennig was in contact with Communists, a suspicion which was soon proved to be false. Claire's religious affiliation aroused particular suspicion. There is a handwritten note on a small piece of A6 paper in the Military Archives bearing no identification of the writer:

> Dr. Johannes Hennig: a German. Here 2 weeks before the war. Claims his wife is a Jewess, but she is not. Comes from Aachen. Staying with Dyer, an officer in the L.S.F. at Sutton (Carramore, The Borough). Very suspect. [*further down, in different handwriting*] arrd. 6.10.39. Age 29. Dr. Phil. Teaching Belvedere College. Address given Belvedere Hotel Gt. Denmark Street. Wife arrd. 22/11/39. Age 33 Wife address 11, Copeland Av., Clontarf.[66]

In 1942 Hennig was still of interest to the Irish authorities. In the Hennig File at the Military Archives, there is a handwritten note from 2 February on 'Hennig – Sutton': 'A friend who has been on visiting terms with the above told me "it is a meeting place for many Germans" including Sachs of TCD and Bieler'.

On the same piece of paper there is a further handwritten note stating 'Sachs / Bieler – both ok as far as known'. However, 1942 was also the year in which Hennig drew attention to himself on account of his publications. This time he came into conflict with the Censorship Board due to an article he wrote for an English journal. It drew attention, it seems, because of his mild criticism of Germany and its allies. The article was intercepted by the mail censors and forwarded by the censorship authorities in Dublin Castle[67] with the following letter from T. Coyne to J.E. Duff of the Department of Justice:

> 9 Meitheamh, 1942
>
> Dear Duff,
>
> Please see the attached papers which include a letter which has been intercepted by the Postal Censorship containing a contribution from Herr Dr. John Hennig to the Catholic Times, London. I know Hennig myself and took German lessons from him and he is, as far as I know, a perfectly harmless alien. At the same time I feel that aliens of German nationality who have left the Fatherland should be discouraged from carrying on anti-Axis propaganda even of so mild a kind as this contribution from here through the medium of the English press. In a previous case (your reference 69/80/93)[68][67] you served an Order on another alien prohibiting him from writing for publication. I don't think it is necessary to go quite so far in this case but, perhaps, you would take some action short of this, such as warning Hennig off the English papers. We have no objection to his occasional contributions on various topics of non-controversial kinds to Irish publications.
>
> Yours sincerely, (So -?) Thomas J. Coyne[69]

It is worth noting that Thomas Coyne knew Hennig personally, had taken German lessons from him and regarded him as harmless, but nevertheless found a warning necessary. The article in question was not published and was, as far as we know, never received by the editor. Duff agreed with the assessment and arranged 'to have him warned in the manner suggested by you'.[70] This restriction of his freedom to publish affected Hennig greatly, and he attempted to have this ban on publishing in English journals lifted. On 24 June 1942 he wrote directly to the Minister for Justice:

A Chara,

The Alien Officer has communicated to me the warning regarding my contributions to British periodicals.

Whilst apologizing for all the inconvenience I have caused in this matter, I would like to point out that all my contributions to the Catholic press in England dealt with religious subjects exclusively, and that only in one case where the editor of a paper had appealed to Catholics to discuss a controversial subject, I sent a contribution, which incidentally was not printed. Otherwise I have never been interested in writing on controversial subjects. My contributions to the press are confined to religious subjects, resulting mainly from the research on liturgy, in which I am engaged for some years past. Fr. Stephan Brown, S.J. Miltown Park, Dublin, Fr. Casey, Editor *The Irish Rosary*, or Mr. O'Curry, Editor *The Standard*, would be able to testify that I am a specialist in that line. It is mainly due to my publications in the Catholic Press of England (*The Universe, The Catholic Herald, Catholic Times, Blackfriars*, and *Music and Liturgy*) that I have succeeded in getting articles published in U.S.A., a fact which is of great importance with a view to my eventual emigration to America. Moreover, those occasional contributions are a small but valuable source of income for me.

It would be a very severe handicap to me if I would be no longer permitted to contribute articles on liturgical subjects to the Catholic press in England, and I would be most grateful if the Minister for Justice would mitigate his warning to that effect that, whilst being prohibited to contribute in controversial subjects, I may continue contributing articles on religious subjects.

Mise, le meas,

J. Hennig

Whether possible emigration to the USA was considered in earnest at this point remains unclear, but his argument that he would lose an important source of income by not being allowed to publish articles in England was certainly of considerable importance to Hennig. After a further exchange of letters between Duff and Coyne, Hennig was granted permission.[71] Hennig went on the offensive for his next publication – he sent it directly to the Department of Justice in the clear hope of saving time:

Since I fear that my letter and the title of my article may give the misleading impression that I am dealing with a controversial political subject, I would like to point out that I am exclusively concerned with a liturgical and historical subject. In order to avoid any delay which otherwise might have been caused, I take the liberty of sending you the letter and article, and I would be grateful if you would kindly forward it in the enclosed envelope.[72]

Duff subsequently sent the letter and article to Coyne (perhaps one can detect a certain exasperated tone in the letter he enclosed: 'If you see no objection to the issue of the enclosure, perhaps you would send it on direct as we do not wish to see it again'[73]), who then passed it on to Joseph Walshe,[74] who also had no objections. Coyne subsequently informed Duff on 1 September that the article could be sent to *The Tablet* without any alterations.

Various Professional Activities

From the beginning of his time in Ireland, Hennig tried to supplement his family income not only with money earned from school teaching and publications, but also by giving private lessons in German. At the beginning of the forties especially, he frequently placed many advertisements in various daily papers, for example: 'German Intensive Courses by experienced Native Teacher – Dr. Hennig, 28 Parnell Square' in the *Irish Times* on 13 and 15 January 1941. In the academic years 1943–44, 1944–45 and 1945–46 Hennig was employed as a part-time lecturer in the seminary at Maynooth and taught German every week during term time.[75] In addition, he gave talks on the radio and evening courses and lectures. For example, in February 1943 he gave a series of six lectures dealing with the place of the 'Missal in the Liturgy, with special reference to the Liturgy of Lent'. The family had settled in, and the two older children, Gabriele and Monica, attended the Santa Sabina pre-school and primary school. From 24 November 1942 a third child joined the flock – Margaret Mary Joan ('Margie').[76] Contact with the neighbours was also good. People remember Hennig as diligent and engrossed in his work, 'friendly scholar who had a good way with children'.[77] In 1943 he started a degree in architecture at University College Dublin, which he did not continue after 1945 partly due to the fact, among other things, that he would have to sit a mathematics examination (*Autobiography*, 153). In 1945 there were further changes and unforeseen professional pressures on Hennig. In March 1945 the death of his friend Hans Sachs affected the Hennig family greatly. The end of the war on the other hand did not constitute a major turning point in the life of the Irish people. Ireland had officially been neutral between 1939 and 1945 and therefore was hardly affected by the war, and if so, then mostly indirectly,[78] for example, through rationing. For Hennig himself the end of the war meant that he was no longer able to continue giving additional German lessons at University College Dublin; and his job at the *Standard* was also terminated (*Autobiography*, 153). In September 1945 the Dun Laoghaire Vocational Education Committee took him on as a part-time teacher; which at least helped in part to compensate for the loss of income from other sources.

Around this time, the Hennigs also considered adopting children from Bergen-Belsen. Dr. Robert Collis,[79] who had treated their daughter Gabriele free of charge when she became extremely ill shortly after their arrival in Ireland, was one of the first Allied doctors to arrive in Bergen-Belsen after the war. In *Die bleibende Statt* Hennig mentions that Collis took a few children from the concentration camp to Dublin. Hennig also describes how he was supposed to find out the religious affiliation of one of the children. He does not mention there that he and Claire thought long and hard about adopting one of these children. Felix Meyer strongly advised them against it.[80] Even though they did not end up adopting a child, John and Claire cared for those children who arrived in Ireland from the concentration camp and, for example, invited them for meals.

On 22 September 1945 the following notice appeared in the *Irish Press*:

> Notice of application of naturalisation
>
> Notice is hereby given that PAUL GOTTFRIED JOHANNES HENNIG, of 'Walmer' Sutton, Co. Dublin is applying to the Minister for Justice for a certificate of naturalisation, and that any person who knows any reason why a certificate of naturalisation should not be issued to the applicant should send a written and signed statement of the facts to the Secretary, Department of Justice, Dublin[81]

Since there were evidently no public objections, in January John Hennig became a 'New Irish Citizen'.[82] The Hennigs had settled down well in Ireland, and there was seemingly never any question of returning to Germany, particularly after what emerged about the horrors of the concentration camps.

In July 1946 came the long-awaited visit of Felix and Marguerite Meyer. Felix Meyer's revealing letter to his other daughter Margot in Switzerland gives a detailed insight into the living conditions of the Hennig family:

We are totally happy and thrilled to be here. And if we didn't have four lovely children in Switzerland, we would gladly remain here forever. Everything is great. Kläre and Hans are wonderful and the three small girls are happy beyond belief. Your mum will tell you all the details. The only worry is that Kläre is trying too hard to make our stay here as pleasant as possible. She is a wonderful host and Hans is too. We are staying with the children, because the thing with the bungalow didn't work out, and naturally it makes family life more congested than if we were just seeing each other now and then. This obviously places great restrictions on Hans and Kläre. The fact that Hans almost always works at home also means that one sees a lot of each other. The children know lots of people, all of them very nice. Almost every afternoon and evening there is someone visiting. They play music, and the two grown-up daughters are always there and never disturb anyone. Our whole life here is so free and easy-going like we have never known it before. Everyone does what he wants. The little children have a glut of friends. All the neighbours' children are in this place or the other, in the sand, in the garden, in houses and in the neighbours' houses, without any adult looking after them. When it is mealtime, the children are called and they come from one house or the other or out of the water or garden. There are often other children there as well at mealtimes, for example, a group of children from Bergen who came to Ireland via Sweden and are to be adopted by Irish families here. The grown-ups have a large number of friends from all backgrounds, some are emigrants with whom they shared the most difficult years.

Hans is one of the best-known men in the country with, in my opinion, a great future ahead of him. He combines immense knowledge with modesty, a gigantic capacity for work, a flair for entertaining, cheerfulness and an easy-going nature with incredible skills round the house. He busies himself about the kitchen and with housework, brings food from the city centre, constantly gives lessons in the most diverse circles, writes for countless magazines and papers, has published several books and is well known and respected. Kläre is naturally hospitable. She has never been so charming as she is now. The difficult years which they both endured have made her more mature and stronger. Kläre is very healthy. Hans, unfortunately, is plagued a lot by headaches so Kläre worries about him. In one or two years they both hope that they will have an easier life. At the moment, I am encouraging him to change his occupation and put it on a more steady footing with more prospects for the future. I would like him to set up a publishing house. This way, he can earn much more than by writing for other newspapers, and he has so much material, that he can fill his own columns for years to come with his own articles and essays. He can find as much money as he wants and technical staff can easily be found. He is still hesitating. His friend, De Valera's closest colleague who himself owns a newspaper, is coming this evening for dinner and we want to ask him about it. I hope Hans doesn't delay long and that the thing will be set up while I am still here and can advise him. That is not to say that he needs me as an advisor. I just have to encourage him and he has to speak honestly with me. Then he could afford staff and a car, and he would have an easier life and wouldn't be so footloose and an exploited writer of articles. I am devoted to seeing him become self-sufficient.[83]

'De Valera's closest colleague' mentioned by Felix Meyer was Frank Gallagher,[84] long-time editor of the *Irish Press*, special adviser to de Valera and Director of the 'Government Information Bureau'. Thanks to Gallagher Hennig was one of the first applicants to be granted Irish citizenship after the war (*Autobiography*, 144). But the envisaged independence did not materialize in the way that Felix Meyer would have wished. There was nevertheless a fairly drastic change in Hennig's professional career. In response to an advertisement in a newspaper, Hennig applied to the state-owned peat-extraction company, Bord na Móna, who were looking for a 'Records Officer with knowledge of German and French'. He took the job offered to him in Newbridge, County Kildare, some 40 miles from Dublin. Relieved to have a permanent job which at least guaranteed a steady income, he wrote a card to his brother Karl at the beginning of December 1946: 'My employment with Bord na Móna has meanwhile been officially confirmed. A full-time job, thanks be to God'.[85]

For the next three and a half years, he was only at home with his young family at weekends. Whilst Felix Meyer had written as late as 1946 that Hennig worked at home a lot,[86] by December 1947 Hennig's sister Erica, who had visited Dublin, wrote that he was almost never at home[87] but rather in Newbridge. Of his time in Newbridge Hennig said, 'I try to brighten up my evenings in the bleak office by writing letters, and also to save time for my precious hours in Sutton'.[88]

It was a tedious job (an 'awful stamp-licking job',[89] as he himself cynically described it), which nevertheless kept his young family provided for, but did not offer him any long-term professional satisfaction, nor did it satisfy his academic capabilities and intellectual needs.

Hennig's workplace is described in a passage from the book *Bord na Móna – Peat Research Centre*:

> The Experimental Station was comprised of five sections. In the Library and Records Section the plentiful and ever-increasing flow of foreign peat handbooks, scientific papers and patents that became available after the war was acquired and indexed by John Hennig who translated and made them available not only to Bord na Móna staff but to Irish industry in general. He also started issuing summaries at regular intervals of current peat research reports that, entitled 'Peat Abstracts', later became a publication with a worldwide circulation.[90]

The Director of Bord na Móna at the time, C. S. Andrews, wrote appreciately of Hennig in his memoir *Man of no Property*:

> As a starting point for these investigations (i.e. 'the study and testing of new natural and artificial drying methods') a comprehensive study was made of world literature on current turf production and utilisation techniques and the latest advances in machine design. Much of this desk research was the work of John Hennig, a German who left Germany because of the Nazi regime. With his remarkable grasp of foreign languages, he built up a comprehensive library and information service, establishing connections with practitioners in bog work in many countries.[91]

The high esteem and regard was reciprocated. Hennig, for his part, saw Andrews as the outstanding representative of a new generation of 'enthusiastic, but economically hard-headed Irish patriots' (*Autobiography*, 160).

In the journal *Architectural Design*, which published a special edition about Ireland, Hennig is described as 'an eminent scientist in charge of technical research'.[92] Hennig made the best of the situation; at least his job gave him the time to pursue his academic studies, even if it was to a lesser extent because he was far removed from a sizeable library and regular exchange of ideas. He engrossed himself especially in Jaspers's monumental work *Von der Wahrheit* (About Truth), which his philosopher friend had sent him, and researched the *Berichte der Antiquarischen Gesellschaft* (Reports of the Antiquarian Society). In his autobiography Hennig vividly reports his experiences over a period of more than three years in Newbridge and his insights into the narrow, provincial life and 'abysmal despair of a small Irish town' at that time. He writes from the perspective of an immigrant German about the country that granted him asylum, towards which he undoubtedly felt fondness and gratitude, but which he did not view uncritically.

For Hennig, life was a daily battle (despite the fact that he had realised since arriving in Ireland that it is better to work to live, than vice-versa, *Autobiography* 177). There was a continuous struggle to fulfil his duties toward Claire and his daughters as far as was humanly possible. He had of course already been shaped by the sacrifice and enormous thriftiness of his parents. Boisterousness and a relaxed cheerfulness were not really his strong points, his was more a dry humour.[93] In a letter dated early 1947, his father-in-law Felix Meyer adressed him in friendly, though emphatic terms:

> Nothing touched me more during our visit than the assertion that you are not enjoying being happy any more. I am pleased about anything erratic you do and any light relief you afford yourselves. You cannot change the fact that it is minus 20 degrees in Berlin. People in Berlin don't freeze any more or any less if it is warm and comfortable and not extreme in your house. You have had so many infinitely hard years behind you that you owe it to yourselves and your children to more contented, to always be contented and well-balanced, even if something goes wrong. [...] Take it from monks [Monica]! Do something which makes you happy! Taking it easy is far more important and of far greater value to the body and soul than a bloody sense of duty. [...] Dear Hans, when I think of how tense you were the first few days we were there and about the little things which you got so annoyed about, the food and the thriftiness and the battle not to waste anything, it makes me very sad. I only wish you would give up your fanatical attitude once and for all. Happiness is essential, more essential than anything else. I have to repeat it again and again. Don't take life so seriously. I must be quite frank, don't expect so much from the hereafter, take more from this life! You have bouts of cheerfulness and both of you certainly have the talent to make yourselves happy. You should develop this talent and neglect the other talents that you may have.[94]

Two years later, a similar letter arrived on Hennig's birthday:

> My dear dear Hans! As a birthday present I assure you in writing that we quite like you. Your wife and children aren't distasteful to us either [...] and I would like to give you as a birthday present a positive outlook on life [...] You will not make things better for anyone else in the world by scavenging for bread or potatoes in the rubbish bin. Lessons from a father to his dear son![95]

This represented the coming together of two very different views on life, each strengthened due to respective experiences during the war years. Hennig was certainly no *bon vivant* who would take things easy, and furthermore, his difficult life as an emigrant had clearly left its mark.

The fact that his family life and work in the library continued to be restricted to the weekend and that he spent long lonely evenings doing 'incommensurable tasks' took their toll. 'It can't go on like this' was Hennig's general reaction (*Autobiography*, 161). His work contract with Bord na Móna also drew to an end. An alternative presented itself in the form of a job offer with another state owned company, the Electricity Supply Board (ESB). Hennig held a similar position to the one in Bord na Móna, that of librarian in their head office in central Dublin.

The job with the ESB meant that there were some positive changes. He was closer not only to his family, but also to his academic sources. Finishing work regularly at 5pm and the central location of his workplace allowed Hennig to undertake some serious research in Dublin's libraries. Hans Reiss, who as a young man went as an exile to Ireland and later became Professor of German in Bristol, recalls:

> I often saw him in either the Reading Room of Trinity College Library or in the National Library. He worked hard, was very diligent and seemed to work in a very

concentrated and systematic fashion; he almost always had a little box of index cards with him.[96]

Around this time, Hennig made the acquaintance of the theatre critic and chronicler Joseph Hone, who in turn introduced him to Arland Ussher (author of *Face of Ireland*) and to his own cousin, the artist Evie Hone. Joseph Hone had invited Hennig to contribute to the 'Dictionary of Irish Writers' which was planned by Hone and Lennox Robinson. Of the fifty articles Hennig subsequently wrote only one was ever published since the lexicon project did not progress beyond the letter 'C'. (*Autobiography*, 167).

While working in Newbridge, Hennig had still managed to maintain his academic contacts to some degree. In recognition of his continued academic activity, Hennig was considered as a candidate for the Royal Irish Academy in early 1947. In his 'Certificate of Candidate' for the Royal Irish Academy, his list of qualifications includes nine essays (a few of which concern Irish-German relations),[97] as well as his dissertation and two articles which he had published in 1936 in Germany. Among those who supported his candidature for the Academy were the Celtic Scholar Gerard Murphy, the classical philologist Micheal Tierney ('from personal knowledge') as well as J. H. Delargy, Erwin Schrödinger, and Arthur Cox, the lawyer mentioned in *Die Bleibende Statt*.[98] Ludwig Bieler and John Hennig were mentioned in a memo on 10.2.1947, which lists them as the candidates up for election. On 15.3.1947, Bieler became a Member of the Academy. It took Hennig a little longer; his name was put forward on 16.2.1948 and simultaneously recommended by the Council of the Academy. On 16 March, he was proclaimed to be a new member and signed the members' list a month later.

Despite the great admiration Felix Meyer had accumulated over the years for Hennig's enormous knowledge ('It's amazing to be such an all-round genius')[99], Meyer was also critical of

Hennig's concentration on academic work, because he believed that Hennig could make more profitable use of his talent for writing and could 'write short stories'.[100] Hennig was aware of his specific talents, but also saw his own limitations. He felt for example, that he lacked the vocabulary and the lightness of touch such as of William Saroyan in *Human Comedy*.[101]

The unexpected death of Felix Meyer on 14 April 1950 must have affected Hennig greatly, especially as their relationship was becoming ever closer and more trusting. As well as the great personal loss suffered by him and his wife, it also meant that from now on Hennig had to be responsible for the affairs of the Rota company, which had benn relocated to Säckingen, Germany at the end of the war. In addition the family had now to care for Marguerite Meyer who moved for a short time to the family home in Sutton. They had been discussing the possibility of buying their own house since 1949 (Felix Meyer had very much recommended it). In the end, the Hennigs bought a house on the Kilbarrack road in Sutton, a few kilometres from Burrow Road. Marguerite lived for a time in the house opposite. The increased commitment to family and business matters finally led to the Hennig family moving to Basel in 1956, from where Hennig again took over the management of the factory. Every day he crossed the Swiss-German border to work, but a complete return to Germany would have been unimaginable for the family.

As well as the feeling of being bound to honour the memory of his father-in-law, there were also other reasons for the family eventually leaving Ireland and moving to the continent. Thoughts about their three daughters' futures played a role, as did the wish to give them wider options for further education and a choice of partner.

The Years in Switzerland

According to statements from his daughter Monica, in Switzerland Hennig's main concern outside professional and family activities was his research. The move to Switzerland opened up the prospect of getting published in German to a far greater extent than before. However, as far as subject matter was concerned, he remained attached to Ireland for a long time. He also continued publishing works relating to Goethe, historical-philosophical questions and particularly liturgical topics. He was also interested in linguistic-philosophical questions and the history of ideas. His contact with the Centre for Liturgical Science in Maria Laach increased over the years; in 1967 Hennig was elected as an extraordinary member of the Abt-Herwegen-Institute for Liturgical and Monastical Research.

On 14 January 1971, Hennig officially became a Swiss citizen. Settling down in Switzerland was not without its problems in the first few years. Once again there was a clear separation between his professional duties, i.e. running the Rota firm, to which Hennig travelled every day, and his family life and his research. The financial security of his family had finally ceased to be a problem, but Hennig continued to spend most of his working week at a salaried job which did not interest him. On top of this there was the difficulty of trying to settle into Basle. Hans Reiss remembers meeting Hennig between the years 1958–1962, when Hennig complained of being regarded as an 'Usländer' (foreigner).[102]

Hennig did, however, have contact with like-minded people, even if they were not as many as he might have hoped. After moving to Switzerland, Hennig once again enjoyed a closer relationship with Karl Jaspers than had been possible during the war and the subsequent years in Ireland. Jaspers had given guest lectures in Basel since July 1947 and in Spring 1948 accepted a permanent post. Hennig contributed an essay entitled 'Karl Jaspers Attitude towards History' to the volume

The Philosophy of Karl Jaspers. The personal contact between the two families remained so close that Gertrud and Karl Jaspers were invited as guests to the wedding of Hennig's daughter Monica to Dian Schefold. In 1970, one year after Jaspers' death, Hennig received an Honorary Doctorate from the Faculty of Philosophy of Basle University in recognition of his academic achievements. Hans Saner, the editor of Jaspers's articles,[103] mentions that Jaspers perhaps had some 'indirect posthumous influence' on the awarding of the Honorary Doctorate. According to Saner Jaspers was very impressed by John Hennig's work and creative capacity:

> He admired him as an excellent scholar on Goethe and a superior historical philosopher and researcher of liturgy. From time to time, there appear to have been disagreements about religious philosophical questions. Jaspers loved debating and arguing and admired the people with whom he could argue.[104]

In Basel, Hennig also had contact with the literary historian Karl Pestalozzi, who in a letter to Hennig thanked him for his essay collection *Literatur und Existenz* and he expressed his admiration 'for the great breadth of your interest and for the great attention to detail, which is often time-consuming in the areas in which you are researching'. Pestalozzi regarded Hennig's work as:

> always strictly objective and at the same time very personal. The fact that Goethe occupies a major part is, therefore, consistent since he always emphasised the importance of recognising the researcher's individuality in the research itself.[105]

Hennig's essays in the above mentioned collection were reproduced in their original format and thereby also reflected in each case the respective historical background of their original production. Pestalozzi refers to this when he says that he has not yet seen a book:

> which brought together essays of different typographical appearance. That lends it a particular charm. The diverse backgrounds thus become evident and every work assumes the aura of its period. I don't know how one could better express the internal authenticity in the layout of the book, although more mundane considerations probably brought it about.

Hennig had also asked Pestalozzi whether Goethe's anniversary in 1982 was to be celebrated in Basle, whereupon Pestalozzi discussed the matter with colleagues and the Rector of the University. Hennig was subsequently invited to participate in a series of lectures being held in the University to commemorate the 150th anniversary of Goethe's death. He chose a theme which was very close to his heart – 'Goethe's knowledge of the non-German European World' (one can safely assume that Ireland played an important role in this).[106] In his later years, Hennig's work on liturgical matters came second to his work on Goethe. And at the age of seventy he still presided over the fate of the firm as well as doing his academic work.

On 16 December 1986 John Hennig died of a tumour in his chest which an operation some years previously had failed to cure. Five years before his death Hennig wrote to his brother Karl that he was afraid of all encounters with his past, and cited Dublin as an example.[107] He never again returned to Ireland after moving to Switzerland. Nevertheless, according to his daughter Monica who was with him in his last hours, one of the last sentences that he spoke on his death bed was: 'The Irish are an especially gifted people because they continuously speak a foreign language'.[108] His thoughts very often returned to Ireland.

John Hennig (in Switzerland he had retained the Anglicised form of the name which he had adopted) asked that his body be cremated. The urn with his ashes was laid to rest in the communal grave of Hörnli graveyard in Basle. Nothing marks the spot. Claire Hennig was also laid to rest here after her death in 1990. The choice of a communal grave originated from their wish to be identified with those many nameless people who died in the Holocaust. A gravestone bearing their initials was not what they wanted.

Hennig's early experience of having to cope on his own probably contributed to his independence and his single-minded determination to pursue his own goals: he followed his own convictions in all aspects of life – an attitude which is reflected in his private, religious, political and professional decisions. However, remaining true to his ideals and holding deep religious beliefs did not lead to an altogether satisfying and fulfilled life. Despite his countless successes and the various honours bestowed on him, such as his acceptance into the Royal Irish Academy, the Honorary Doctorate in Basel and his success in providing for his family under the most difficult of conditions time and time again, he had the feeling that his real work – his research and countless publications – never met with the attention they deserved. Shortly before his seventieth birthday, he heard of his brother Karl's plans to write another book, and replied: 'I am gradually losing the courage and strength [...] since I know nobody who would be interested in it'.[109] In hard times, it was above all his family who helped him.[110] All the same – the political circumstances in Germany, which prevented his professional career from developing along the lines that corresponded to his interests and ability, and the enforced period of exile, prompted John Hennig to make the following statement towards the end of his life: 'It [being a convert] does not alter the fact that I am uprooted, not only socially, professionally, politically and linguistically, but also in religion' (*Autobiography*, 211). But he ended his autobiography on a conciliatory note and said that as a convert, foreigner and non-professional he indeed suffered constraints, but on the other hand had also enjoyed exceptional freedom of movement. In our context, there is yet another reason to come to a positive conclusion: without the 'uprooting' of John Hennig, which tore him out of the German academic context, we would not have his many personal observations in the sphere of German-Irish relations. The story of 'Irlandkunde' (Irish area studies), a term Hennig first coined, would certainly be a different one, and it is doubtful whether German-Irish studies would be as advanced as they are today.

Gisela Holfter and Herman Rasche

In John Hennig's autobiography *The Lasting Abode* (*Die bleibende Statt*, privately published, Bremen 1987) the two chapters relating to his experiences in Ireland are published here for the first time in an English translation.

WAR

As I crept down the stairs in the grey of morning, there was a knock at the door. Another telegram. The Refugee Committee in Dublin informed me that my visa had been issued and could be collected in Paris. These good people had forgotten that my family was in much greater danger than I, and that it was hardly feasible to collect the visa after the outbreak of the war. The obliviousness of the fortunate and the healthy, the rich and the successful, has always haunted me. Years later, I was to visit a woman suffering from tuberculosis. I said to her, 'there is no point in trying to encourage you, because you will simply answer, "but you haven't got tuberculosis"'. 'You are the first sensible person to visit me', she said, 'and you have helped me more than any words of comfort'.

I cabled to Dublin, asking what would happen to my family. Their answer: I should come over first; the rest could be sorted out later. Only much later did I realise that this type of answer in the English-speaking world is equivalent to the most eloquent confirmation elsewhere. A smuggler was willing to travel to Paris with my German passport and collect the visa, in return for what had become for us a huge sum of money. I prayed through two sleepless nights. The passport could well be more valuable to the smuggler than his reward. My father-in-law simply coerced me to have faith, and as usual he was right.

Once on the ship, we were fortunately distracted by learning how to put on the life jackets so that there was no time to watch the disappearing coastline. When we landed at Folkestone, a Jewish man took his life after being prevented from leaving the ship. I was led into the immigration office along with another family. The husband's name was called out first: 'Schrodinger'. 'Forgive me if I ask a stupid question', I said when he came back, 'but would you be the great Schrodinger?' 'Whether or not I am great, I don't know', he answered. 'I am a physicist, and like you, I am travelling on to Dublin'. It must be a good omen, I thought, to emigrate in such good company. With a touching lack of concern, considering it was in the early days of the war, we were allowed to wander freely around London. I went to Westminster Cathedral and prayed at the altar of St. Patrick, under whose protection I now placed myself.

In Dublin, I was protected from idle dreaming by the objectivity so characteristic of the Jesuits. On the morning after my arrival, I was already teaching. 'I must tell you, as you are German, we don't believe in working the boys too hard'. This was the only instruction I received. In the schoolyard, a boy stood talking to a priest. He had the loose end of his belt in his hand, and was swinging it about as they obviously told each other jokes. At the beginning of every class, the teacher was expected to kneel down beside the desk and recite a 'Hail Mary'. These were my first impressions. Only the privileged pupils in the two final classes took German – I was dealing with an elite. One of the boys later told me how difficult it had been not to laugh at my limited English.

Thanks to the small advance my father-in-law had pressed upon me, I was able to afford a room in a fourth-rate hotel in the slums. The first cold spell set in; a turf fire burned in the hall of the hotel only in the evenings. I sat at the window in my room looking out on the row of eighteenth-century houses and watching people pass by the school gate and bless themselves, merely because they knew there was a chapel nearby.

A poster on the wall of a house invited people to a mission. I asked the landlady if she could tell me how to find this church. 'That's not a very respectable area', she said. The corrugated-iron building was in the part of the city made famous by James Joyce in *The Portrait of the Artist* and in *Ulysses*. The Legion of Mary's first deed had been to achieve the closure of the brothel there. The girls were invited to take part in spiritual exercises, and they came. The church was filled with people smelling of leek and dripping. Steam rose from the wet woollen clothes worn by rows of women in black shawls. Two Redemptorists ensured an atmosphere of urgency. I later came to understand their technique; one thundered and the other whispered, drenching the faithful alternately in ice-cold and lukewarm water. I was also to become familiar with their little books of anecdotes, which were all supposedly personal and recent experiences. But what did all this mean? No one can truly appreciate the Rosary until he has joined in saying it in a church in the Dublin slums. Whenever I hear the sentimental hymn (now dying out), 'Mother of Christ, Star of the Sea, pray for us sinners, pray for me', I am conscious of the inadequacy of the continental's approach.

My first errand had been to go to the Department of Justice to secure visas for my family. In the lift, a small picture was pinned over the door - a portrait of De Valera perhaps or of some other national hero? No, it was the picture found in every Catholic home in Ireland, the Sacred Heart of Jesus, with the inscription, 'I will bless the house where my image is honoured'. This picture had not been put up in the building by government order, like the holy pictures in Schuschnigg's Austria.

The idea of blessing oneself on walking or driving past a church became second nature to us over the years. Even the tram conductor would raise his cap. When the Angelus rang out at midday or in the evening, people stood still and the men removed their hats. Once I even saw a traffic policeman on his platform take off his helmet; in all four directions, the traffic waited patiently. In the National Library, some readers would kneel down beside their desks for the Angelus, and no one took any notice. In offices, the typewriters would cease to clatter and in schools, the lessons would be interrupted. If one happened to be paying a visit at that moment, the host might well say to his guest: 'Let us say The Angel of the Lord ...'

People prayed without embarrassment not only with each other but for each other as well. Whenever people in need were told, 'I wish I could do something for you', they would answer, 'But of course you can, you can pray for me'. On special occasions in Ireland, one would present the person with a whole bouquet of prayers. These were often worked out almost mathematically but still involved a great deal of effort. My mother said she was thankful for all her sleepless nights, because they gave her time to pray for those in need.

An Irish friend once told me, 'Something sad happened to me today. I went into a church today and found Our Lord completely alone'. This actually happened very rarely. Apart from prayers of thanksgiving and prayers of petition – particularly for others – the prayer of worship was also popular. 'Dropping in' was part of the daily routine for thousands. Shoppers would steam into the Carmelite Church just off the main street in the city centre to spend a few minutes.

On the first evening in our new flat, I heard voices murmuring through the thin walls. After a while I realised the whole family next door was saying the Rosary together. In Ireland, the mystery is mentioned before each decade. The custom of inserting it as a relative clause in each Hail Mary would be considered as Teutonic meticulousness. On the other hand, people on the continent cannot conceive the faithful praying continuously from midday on November 1st to the evening of souls from purgatory nor of their reciting 1500 Hail Mary's in 72 hours, as they do during the pilgrimage to Lough Derg. I realised how impossible it was to convey the reality of Ireland to people elsewhere. A well-known Belgian Catholic once told me, 'Les Irlandais sont très superstitieux'. It takes four weeks as a tourist in Ireland to write a book about the secrets of the Emerald Isle, a few years to write an article on 'My experiences in Dublin' and anyone who has spent 17 years there prefers to remain silent.

I obtained permission to augment my 'salary' from Belvedere College up to a maximum of one pound per week by giving private lessons. My first pupil was an elderly spinster, a sales assistant in a department store, who was one of the few Irish Catholics opposed to Germany winning the war. She wanted to learn French – I had boldly claimed that I could teach that as well – in order to go to Lourdes some day. In her prayers she had asked the mother of God whether she could take lessons from a German. Orphaned early, she lived in unspeakably dreary 'digs', the last refuge for single people. When she asked me what she should do, I burst out, 'Try to become a saint'. She slapped her hands. 'Yes, that's it', she cried. 'the Holy Ghost is a pet, he gives me everything'.

The outward misery of church life in Ireland is aggravated by the fact that almost all of the older churches, not destroyed during the

Reformation, are in Protestant hands. In Dublin, the Catholic Pro-Cathedral was crowded with church-goers on Sundays, with Masses every half-hour between 6 and 12 and often several masses being read at side altars simultaneously, whereas only small groups of Anglicans trooped to the one or two services at the two medieval cathedrals. The newer churches, with the exception of the classical Pro-Cathedral, were indescribably ugly. The worst of these were the most recent ones, where the mediocrity of the new affluence expresses itself in marble statues, floors and ornamentation. At that time, 85% of the Catholics went to Mass every Sunday, 70% fulfilled their Easter obligation, 50% went to confession once a month, and 30% once a week in order to receive Communion daily; 95% did not eat meat on Fridays. We had to revise our preconceived notions dramatically. In the Pro-Cathedral on Christmas Eve, there were two rows of up to thirty people waiting for each of the ten confessionals: the doors of the confessionals slid across every minute. Spiritual guidance was possible at other times particularly in the churches of the religious orders. There, there was only the boundless desire to be at peace with God. Only people who have never witnessed the intensity of this desire could possibly speak of absolution machines.

The other side of the coin is easier to perceive. The servile mentality caused by centuries of unprecedented repression, addiction to alcohol and gambling, aversion to work, cheating and swindling, unreliability in human relationships, deadly routine, the most despicable perversions, and hypocrisy – we were not spared any of this. Yet it all faded to insignificance in the face of our inexpressible gratitude towards the country that alone had saved our lives and allowed our children to grow up in peace. Humanity reached far beyond confessional differences.

During the first months, we hadn't enough clothing to survive a cold, wet winter in a tiny flat. My wife and the two children fell ill with whooping cough – still incurable at the time. Our eldest daughter developed a lung complication. The landlady first suggested whiskey as a remedy, then water from Lourdes. When the child appeared to be lost, we turned to the city's best-known paediatrician, Dr. Collis. He did everything to save our daughter's life without charging a penny. She owes her life to him.

This doctor was later one of the first to reach Bergen-Belsen with the Allies, and he brought a number of children back to Ireland where adoptive parents were sought. In the case of an eight-year-old girl, they were not sure whether or not she was Jewish. As a Protestant, the doctor suggested that the child be examined by a Catholic, and as the child spoke some German, I was asked. I took her to a church, but there was no sign of recognition at the sight of a crucifix. I reported that it seemed to me unlikely that the child was Catholic. Our local doctor, a Catholic, said to me, 'That was not the answer the committee expected. You are an honest man'. These words remained in my memory not because I thought them justified but because they were the beginning of a friendship. This doctor had often supported me when I felt depressed by narrow-mindedness. I heard such good jokes from him about priests, jokes that could only have been told by someone with a very deep love of the Church.

At the critical time when my daughter was ill, I was offered a job as a tutor of a noble family in the west of Ireland. In the space of three weeks, I was to prepare two students for the Cambridge examination in German. On the first morning, one of them took me to an ivy-covered ruin near the manor house. We climbed up. 'As far as you can see, this land has belonged to my family since the days of the Normans'. And yet these people were still considered foreigners in Ireland. On Sunday morning, I asked to be allowed to attend Mass at the parish church two miles away. I travelled there on a horse-drawn cart with the servants and a few farm workers. It was the same atmosphere described by another native of Leipzig, Goethe's friend Kuettner, in the first book by a German completely devoted to Ireland.

Despite our reluctance to tap our last financial reserves, we decided for the children's sake to find a new flat. Doors were closed everywhere when we mentioned that we had two small children. Finally, I read an advertisement from the suburb of Sutton, which lies on the spit of land connecting the Hill of Howth (made famous through the final chapter of Joyce's *Ulysses*) with Dublin. The dilapidated little hut was hardly fit for human habitation. On the way back to the railway station, I went into the small corrugated-iron church on the side of the road. While waiting for the next train, I strolled past the hedgerows, looking longingly at the beautiful gardens and exclusive houses leading to the beach. I suddenly decided on a last desperate try and simply knocked at the door of one of the houses claiming I had heard that there was a flat to let. Yes, that was correct. The woman showed me the flat. It was ideal for us, and the rent was reasonable. But we had children. Boys or girls? Two girls. Oh, that was just fine; she was looking for company for her little daughter. Psychologically speaking, it is probably a question of perspective whether coincidences are interpreted as answers to prayers or not. However, after experiencing dozens of these coincidences, one ceases to describe them as such. In my view, this is comparable to the popular belief in St. Anthony, who won't do anything more for you unless you show your gratitude afterwards.

The first summer came. I could hardly restrain my tears when principal of Belvedere College informed me that the two months' summer holidays were of course without pay, and then wished me an enjoyable summer. I immediately followed up each reply to my newspaper advertisements with a personal visit. In one case, I was instantly stuck by a quotation on the wall indicating that my prospective client belonged to the Oxford Group, already familiar to me through the meeting in the Utrecht in 1938 and again through Emil Brunner's consent. During the course of the conversation, it became clear that we both took our respective beliefs seriously. A few days later, he paid us a visit. He and three friends were planning to tour the west of Ireland but all along they had had a hunch that a fifth person was going to join them. Thus it was that I spent a few unforgettable days on the western edge of Europe. One morning, these friends asked me to conduct prayers with them as I was accustomed to doing. In an excellent booklet of liturgical prayers, *The Voice of the Church*, I found a short text in which the phrase 'quiet time' was used (the observation of a 'quiet time' had been recommended by Frank Buchman). We knelt down in the open air, in sight of the sea, and after I had finished reading, the others copied out the prayer for their own use.

Soon, local people began to appear at our campfire in the evenings; people who lived in stone huts they had built themselves between the fields where a few potatoes and some oats were grown in seaweed: people whose staple diet in winter was carrageen Moss and who eked out a meagre living by catching lobsters. Together we sang the spirited songs of the Moral Rearmament Movement, and finished with a prayer. We visited families in their one-room huts, divided in half by the wall where the turf fire always burned with a cauldron or bread-baking pot hanging over it. Having seated us in the place of honour on stools beside the fire, our hosts served us fresh bread sprinkled with sugar on spotless plates, and offered us a drink of milk. An ancient gramophone was played to complete the royal welcome.

A girl from one of the poorest families wrote to me after our return, saying that she had cried when we departed as it had always been so lovely with us. We began to correspond. A year later she ran away with her boyfriend. Today she is the mother of eight children; she had her youngest at the same time her daughter's first child was born. In addition to the weather, the fishing and the children growing up, this woman writes to me about taking part in rosaries, novenas and missions. I have seen her only once in the thirty years intervening, but if I can be sure that any living person is praying for me, then it is she.

The friend who had invited me on this tour accompanied me to Mass on Sunday. The church stood at the top of a crossroad far from any village. Nowhere, not in St. Vitus' Cathedral in Prague, nor the church of Dionysus in Athens, nor the Church of Dormitio in Jerusalem, have I come to realise more clearly how the use of Latin contributed to making the church my home. Those who are so quick today to sweep aside arguments based on tourism and a migrant workforce have obviously never experienced this problem first-hand. In Ireland the introduction of the national language (as in continental Europe and Africa) did not have the desired unifying effect. It was the aim of the government to preserve the Irish Language in the West of Ireland. This was hardly possible in view of the inevitable necessity for young people to emigrate to Britain or America. The rule stating that at least one of the Masses on Sundays or holy days must be in Irish was something of a farce – most people knew even less Irish than they did Latin.

On our last evening, we visited the home of the boy who had supplied us with food and petrol he had prospered when a barrel of acetone was washed ashore from a shipwreck, an extremely rare commodity which he got rid of while evading the customs officers and police. His mother took the unexpected blessing from God without asking awkward questions. She asked us about life in faraway Dublin. As someone from beyond even England, I was regarded as some of exotic animal. She had me kneel down and gave me her special blessing.

Of the four people who invited me along, each belonged to a different church – Methodist, Anglican, Presbyterian and Plymouth Brethren (the more moderate branch, of course, since the stricter branch would not have been allowed to associate with the unclean). The subject of religion obviously took up much of our conversation. For Irish Catholics, the rules regarding *communio in sacris* were particularly strict. Once, when I had gone to the burial service of a Presbyterian friend, a Catholic friend told me that only the Archbishop could absolve me of this mortal sin. Moral Rearmament, to which my four friends belonged, was among the many movements prohibited to Catholics.

I was afraid they thought I was acting under pressure from outside when I didn't join the movement. My reasons for not joining were, however, of a different nature. It was my father's sense of ethics that had made me wary of moral platitudes. The four standards of Moral Rearmament – absolute honesty, absolute purity, absolute selflessness, absolute love – appeared to me to be just as trite as the social policy programmes of today. Nevertheless, the concrete evidence of genuinely ethical behaviour was very impressive indeed. I saw splendid examples of this not only among Quakers but also among members of the Oxford Group.

The only time of year we felt really homesick was Christmas. In most Irish families, Christmas day itself was celebrated with paper streamers, balloons and an unbearably heavy meal. Our new friends from Moral Rearmament showed us that there were other ways of celebrating Christmas, such as inviting the needy to the family meal. Their daughters dedicated their lives to God and were actively involved in the group, demonstrating the enthusiasm with which many small religious communities often put the Church to shame. These friends were of Scottish ancestry, and after the meal they listened with reverence to the King's speech on the radio. George VI will be remembered not as the man who promised his people a thousand year empire, but when many were without hope, he said: 'I went out into the darkness and stretched out my hand'.

What impressed me even more, however, were our friend's efforts on behalf of a poor Catholic family from the West of Ireland. The father worked away from his family in Dublin. One day, he turned up at our friend's office with a frightful hangover. Our friend took him to a church and had him pray there for a while. 'After a short time, I noticed that he had made his peace with God again'. Being well connected, our friend was able to get him a job close to where his family lived. The young man who had taken me to the West of Ireland owned a cottage in the Wicklow Mountains near Dublin. On arriving one day, he found that it had been vandalised. The culprits were apprehended but my friend succeeded in persuading the judge to give them a rather unusual sentence: they had to spend three weekends in the house to build a crib, and then help distribute presents to the poor children of the area at Christmas.

During this time, the wife of a high-ranking civil servant found herself drawn to the Moral Rearmament by their good deeds, just as I had been. She too was a convert. We both found it necessary to defend the group against the suspicions of other Catholics. But we also had to make it clear to our friends in the group that we had chosen a different path.

My experiences with the Legion of Mary were comparable to those of Moral Rearmament. Despite the excellent example of individual members and their friendly generosity, I could not bring myself to join. The invitation to do so came from the highest level. A young private pupil told me enthusiastically of his involvement with the organisation. Like Moral Rearmament, the Legion gives the small man a chance and, with it, self-confidence. At one of the group's meetings, the (dreaded) archbishop arrived unannounced, but he quietly took a seat and business continued. An amateur dramatic performance in the local Legion Hall gave us an idea of what actually happened at these meetings. With Irish irony, typical little mistakes in their work were pointed out: personal vanity, a tendency to gossip, romantic attachments, etc. My young friend introduced me to the Legion's founder, Frank Duff, who was considered a saint by his supporters. When I expressed the reservation that, as a foreigner, I could hardly get involved, he suggested that I found a Catholic underground movement in Nazi Germany. He proposed that I disguise it as a Goethe Society. A more decisive factor was when I told him of a real emergency case of which I had heard. He tried to understand it by drawing a comparison to an outwardly similar case but, in my view, missing the essential point of the case I had outlined. Since my dissertation, I have held the opinion that, although comparison is an almost unavoidable aid to memory, in the spiritual sphere it is ultimately lethal. In the dispute between nomothetic and ideographic conceptions of history, I adhere strongly to the ideographic point of view. I am united with Jaspers in his aversion to nomothetic psychiatry. Ever since my childhood, I have been acutely aware of the insoluble problem of trying to reconcile effective aid and individual needs in charitable work. Duff had unwittingly touched upon a sore point in my life.

Some years later, I was profoundly shocked by the treatment the Legion gave to a young Greek girl who moved into our area. She had been involved with an Irishman serving in the British army, who had deserted her after she had borne him three children. The Legion's principle of helping in every way except materially was diametrically opposed to my experience and perception of reality. In this particular case, the Legion's members did not adhere to this principle rigidly. When the young woman refused to become a Roman Catholic, however, she was talked about in a tone that I found displeasing. She had indeed been somewhat ungracious and even ungrateful, but is it not a case of once bitten twice shy? I also felt that the Greek girl's own church was the last refuge she still had.

I presented Duff with the manuscript of a booklet, which had just been accepted by a Dublin publisher, concerning the history and liturgy of the Festival of Mary Mediatrix of all Graces. He found fault with my translation of the prayers and suggested a version, which, in my opinion, anticipated it being made dogma. I couldn't accept it. Duff was peeved. I could never accept the main objection, which I had always heard made against the Legion, that their way of getting straight to the point was tactless. The question, 'When did you last beat you wife?' is certainly not the worst approach. I found the Legion's constant reports of victory tedious, but then I heard of the martyrdom of the legionaries in China. Whenever I meet such active and self-sacrificing people, it makes me wonder whether it is the lack of commitment generally attributed to intellectuals that holds me back. I was grateful when it became unnecessary to take a stand by exterior circumstances – such as the pressure of work or having to move to another area.

Having spoken only English throughout my trip around the West of Ireland, I now felt in a position to improve my meagre income by some writing. One of the minor magazines circulated by the missionary orders accepted my first article. The fee was ten shillings. A Catholic weekly newspaper, the *Standard* was pleased with some of my other articles and offered to take 1000 words every week. The press reflected the spiritual situation of Catholicism in Ireland. By far the most informative newspaper was the *Irish Times*, a publication with Protestant leanings and a more positive attitude towards England. The weekly newspapers were considered Catholic: the *Standard* tended to be nationalistic, the *Irish Catholic*, devotional. My situation at the *Standard* was embarrassing. The day after the first bombing raid on Coventry, I was congratulated on the brave deeds of my countrymen. I specialised in writing articles on every new country Hitler attacked, including anything which could be said about the situation of the Catholic Church there. I wrote a series of articles about those countries where the Germans had been forced to retreat. It was a macabre affair.

An article for the *Standard* on the state of the Catholic Church in Indo-China provoked a furious letter from a priest whose name, Grat Spreti, made a lasting impression. My information, taken from a book published in 1937, was hopelessly outdated. I apologised to the writer of the letter and explained my situation. I promptly received an invitation to visit him and his community, the Steyler Fathers, in the Irish Midlands.

On two afternoons a week, I was allowed to read the *Neue Zuercher Zeitung*, the *Tat* and the *Schweizer Rundschau* at the Swiss Consulate, and thus had access to news no other newspaper reported. Through meeting the Consul, Dr. Benzinger, and visiting his elegant home, I became acquainted with some of the best qualities of the country where I would one day live. This was at a time when I needed to know that there was somewhere in the world where all was well. Benzinger's superior attitude towards Catholicism in Ireland made me suspect that it would be far from easy were I ever to remove myself from the fascinating hold of this country. However, without the gift I was fortunate to inherit, the ability to see only the good side of a particular set of circumstances. I would not have been able to cope. The gratitude I feel for Ireland is sufficient justification for any lack of objectivity.

My financial position was particularly precarious as I was officially qualified neither for my original job nor for my later business career. In a country with so many unemployed, business activity was impossible as long as I remained a foreigner. My teaching work increased somewhat when I was given a few hours teaching students of German at the National University. On the basis of a personal recommendation – the only time in my life I took advantage of one – I was appointed German assistant at the National Seminary for the priesthood in Maynooth. Shortly before that, I had decided, in my desperation, to begin studying architecture. As I was also delivering a series of lectures at the Central Catholic Library, I would often be concerned from 9 to 12 with the difference between sash windows and casement windows, from 2 to 3 with the difference between benedictions and consecrations, and would end up writing an article in the evening on the relationship between Czechs and Slovacs.

Within the space of a year, my clerical students had just about mastered enough German to tackle the New Testament. I bought the books at the Protestant Bible Society. At the time, I was probably the only Catholic to cross the threshold of this ship. I arranged my trips from Dublin to the college of Maynooth, 20 miles away so that I still had some time to work in the library. Here, as in the National Library, I enjoyed the privilege of direct access to the shelves. I had to make clever use of the limited library facilities in order to further my academic work. My headquarters were Trinity College Library and one of the British copyright libraries, but I depended on other libraries for theological literature. I found out that the first volume of the *Jahrbuch fuer Liturgiewissenschaft* was in the National Library and the other volumes, up to the outbreak of the war, were in Maynooth. I finally discovered a journal, which was very important to me in the Jesuit Library in Rathfarnham. I borrowed a Pontificate and the Concordance to the Vulgate from one of the priests in the order. It took many hours to organise even the most essential documents. My output included booklets in the *Irish Home Handbook Series* (still sold today in

Woolworth's, entitled 'The House Doctor', 'Mother and Child', 'The Brides Book' and 'Modern Youth' for which I received sixty pounds each. I did not hesitate to combine what I had read with personal experience). I also wrote treatises on obscure issues of church history and theology. I sent these at random to journals in Britain, the USA and Canada, often only knowing the name of the periodical. I would have to pay for the offprints myself. An article could be returned up to ten times with a note saying, 'The editor regrets' – often so crumpled that I would have to re-type it. I discovered that among the Celtic philologists, who have no idea about liturgy, and students of liturgy, who regard Ireland as just a part of England, there was still room for someone with partial knowledge of both areas. The Celtic scholar, Gerard Murphy, contacted me upon reading my treatise about the Feast of All Saints of Europe, which was unique to ancient Ireland. I had suggested that old Irish liturgy was based on different perception of time than the Roman – a theory that has since been accepted even by liturgical dictionaries. 'You have made real discovery there' he said. 'You have in fact enabled me to understand our Irish martyrologies for the first time'. Murphy then proposed my admission to the Royal Irish Academy. I was sworn into this illustrious society by its then president, Monsignor Boylan, the great exegete. On one occasion I stood at the table in the Academy's reading room where new acquisitions were on display. There were also two new offprints of mine. I heard one visitor say to another, 'Who is this Hennig anyway?'.

In a sense, I had joined the ranks of the continental specialists on Irish saints – both real and 'supposed' ones, as Louis Gougaud called them – but I placed the study of this field in a wider context, unlike most people working on this subject. I was not interested in the historicity of the saints, but in tradition, particularly as representative or expressive of continental 'Irish Studies' (Irlandkunde). I coined this phrase in deliberate contrast to my distant relative Walter Hofstaetter's phrase, 'German Studies' (Deutschkunde), and I am pleased that it has since been used in the title of a university institute. Nobody has probably researched the history of continental, particularly German, Irish Studies as extensively as I have. Their sporadic nature made them suitable for treatment in literary magazines, the only medium open to me. This theme is a sad illustration of the astonishing continentocentrism of the Catholic world, particularly the unwillingness to recognise that basic concepts in our way of thinking do not apply elsewhere. The knowledge that there are people living on the other side of the fence, who are fundamentally different from me and from anything I could ever be, hit home with extraordinary impact in Ireland. Ever since then I cannot suppress a certain annoyance about the casual way today's central European middle classes assume, as a foregone conclusion, that their standards alone are valid.

The few who encouraged me in my literary work (the proceeds of which saved my family from the worst) were exceptional people. Ludwig Bieler had come to Ireland at the same time as we had, and for the same reasons. Having become known for his work on Irish Church history, he embarked on a modest academic career, which increasingly won him the admiration he deserved in academic circles. He became an authority on St. Patrick, the national saint, and the Director of the National Library entrusted him with the task of collecting information about Irish manuscripts found outside Ireland. Bieler built up the unique microfilm collection of the prints corner of the National Library in Dublin. Our friendship with him and his wife is deeply rooted in faith and willingness to deal with new issues which confront us.

Eoin McNeill, one of the foremost experts on old Ireland was the first to encourage me to study Ireland's relations with early medieval Europe beyond the so-called missionary period usually dealt with in church history. In my studies on young Goethe's occupation with a Celtic language, with MacPherson's 'originals' of Ossian's poetry, he gave me invaluable advice. Thanks to my teacher, Witkowski, I interpreted the numerous references to Ireland in Middle High German literature not as a historical motive, as had been customary so far, but as an expression of knowledge about a remote country, with which there were no physical connections. It was with the presentation of this study that I first introduced myself to the Academy.

Another member of the Academy, who was also my solicitor, Arthur Cox, also took an interest in this paper. He was quite the most extraordinary Irishman I have ever known. Married to the widow of Kevin O'Higgins, the Minister killed by De Valera's supporters in the Civil War. He was an indispensable advisor to the governments of De Valera's party. His office on Stephen's Green looked as if they had come straight from the time of Dickens. Cox always sat in semi-darkness. The only indication that he was listening to you came from his occasional grunt. When he did say something, though, it was pure gold. It was he who first taught me that the best solicitor is the one who avoids litigation as long as possible. He once asked me, 'Do you want to make the man your enemy?' Over the years, this question has often prevented me from doing foolish things. When we were finished with the business side of things, Cox would often invite me to a small café for a cup of tea. Then he would ask, 'So what are you really doing?' He was practically the only one to realise that my academic interests were my 'real' work. There was no subject upon which he could not give a wise and well-informed opinion. By accident, I found out that this busy man spent an hour every day at his ailing mother's bedside. In his sixties, he gave up his thriving practice, joined the Jesuits and went out on the missions to Africa. He died as he lived – victim of an accident while travelling for his work.

Frank Gallagher, well known for his diary of the hunger strike in 1926 (written under the pen name of David Hogan), was De Valera's Minister of Information. Although fully aware that I could never be a true Irishman, Gallagher saw to it that I was among the first to be granted Irish citizenship after the war. I had, for instance, been unable to find the time to follow Gerard Murphy's advice to learn Old Irish and learned only the rudiments of Modern Irish with my children. Gallagher knew, however, that I would never be able to make a decent living without citizenship. This genuine patriot taught me more about recent Irish history than any book. The years of terror had not robbed him of his golden Irish sense of humour. His two adopted daughters were his whole life. Above all, I have rarely seen a person so radiant with natural goodness, demonstrated time and again by his skill as a storyteller.

To illustrate this idiosyncrasy of the Irish, Gallagher was fond of telling a story already preserved in the literature of the penal times, concerning two Irishmen who lie in wait for one of the dreaded English landlords, planning to murder him as he returns from town at night. Ten o'clock, eleven o'clock passes and there is no sound of horses. By half past eleven, one of the Irishman says to anther 'I hope to God nothing's happened to the poor fellow'.

The clergy, who often came to Gallagher's house, were not spared by their host either. Instead of church taxes in Ireland, priests must depend on Christmas and Easter dues, in other words, voluntary donations. Gallagher used to say 'Over two pounds and they would call the donor "Mister" when the donations were being read out in church, over one pound and the family's name would be given, less than that and it would just be "John" or "Peter"'. Another of Gallagher's stories in this context involves a priest in a relatively prosperous village who had difficulty obtaining even the barest minimum from his parishioners. One day, the helper who also served as the sacristan asked if he might be allowed to collect dues. After much consideration, the priest finally yielded. A few days later, notes and cheques began pouring into the presbytery. One envelope, however, also contained a letter which read: 'Reverend Father, please find dues enclosed as requested, but please note that "dirty" is written with an "i" and "blackguard" with only one "g"'.

The differences in character between the true Irish and the English are so great that I cannot wonder enough at the naïvety of continental newspapers and broadcasters who take reports on Ireland from London at face value. Until recently there were basically two types of priests in England, those who were imported from Ireland and those who were born in England, often converts. According to Gallagher, an Irish priest in Liverpool was tired of the dull converts he kept being sent as curates. The bishop wrote in reply to his complaint, saying that he hoped he would find the next curate more satisfactory. The young man was called into the room. 'Convert?', 'Yes'. The priest could not help sighing. 'Cigarette?' 'Yes, thank you'. 'A glass of beer?' 'Why not'. 'A wee dram to go with it?' 'With pleasure'. 'Well, tell me then, my dear fellow, what kept you away from the church for so long?'

And now one last Frank Gallagher story. On her way to Mass, a woman meets a neighbour with whom she does not get on. 'I'm afraid I'm in a state of grace at the moment' she shouts, 'but just wait until I come back from Holy Communion, then I'll give it to you!' A healthy dose of humour would make current criticism of the church far more effective.

Because of its poverty, Ireland could admit very few immigrants. Dr Josef Grabisch, however, remained in Ireland at the outbreak of the war in compliance with the wishes of his American wife. He was not really a true immigrant. He had made a name for himself through his studies on Hamann and Catholic theology, although he had turned away from the Church. His brooding nature and his often abstruse profundity were reminiscent of his compatriot Jakob Boehme. He spent his days scouring the second-hand bookshops on the quays for German books or books relating to Germany. As a matter of principle, he refused to pay more than sixpence for any volume. Quite indiscriminately he collected schoolbooks, classics, travel books and translation. The manuscript of his preliminary research on Mangan's efforts to promote German Classics and Romantic literature among English-speakers is in the National Library in Dublin, still waiting for anyone able to read the old German handwriting.

When it became clear that Germany would lose the war, Grabisch was on the verge of a nervous breakdown. His wife begged me to take him to the country. It seemed a good opportunity to accept the Steyler Fathers' open invitation to spend a few days with them. On our first stroll through the gardens, Grabisch accosted one of the Fathers. 'I don't understand how the Pope can claim celibacy is justified by the Scriptures'. In addition to my study of Hermes and Guenther, my dealings with Grabisch acquainted me with the historical roots of the *aggiornamento*.

The Fathers prayed every quarter of an hour. Day and night the clock chimes, interrupted whatever they were doing - working, lecturing or reading - to allow them to say a short prayer. I ventured to predict that the Fathers would not win over many Irish people with this exacting discipline. But was I right? I joined one of them on his spiritual calls in this very poor area. We entered a half-ruined cottage where a woman was living with her retarded daughter. She belied my prediction by welcoming the priest with the deepest respect and admiration.

The Grabisches were cared for by the Irish people who had taken it upon themselves to save their guests souls. Being very close to Grabisch, we were understandably sceptical when we heard that he had become reconciled with the Church on his deathbed. He will always be remembered by us as one of the just, who earnestly sought the truth. The rest is up to God. His wife was received into the Church after his death, but I never broached religious matters with her. She retained the unapproachable dignity of the aristocracy from the southern states. She and her husband founded a society in Berlin in 1916 to support Roger Casement. It was the short-lived German-Irish Society, supported by Kuno Meyer. Grabisch had a curiously ambivalent attitude towards Ireland. His intense aversion to the Irish language movement was second only to his acute fear of being buried in Irish soil (he thought the clay was poisonous, contrary to the belief expressed in ancient sagas that Irish soil had healing powers). Nationalists erected a Celtic cross on his grave in Dublin, with an Irish inscription.

On another occasion, I had the opportunity of spending a holiday with the Cistercians in Roscrea. I took part in their life of prayer, starting at two o'clock in the morning. The Father in charge of visitors showed great interest in my little essay on the liturgical significance of the veneration of the Heart of Mary. He regarded the recent consecration of the human race to the Heart of Mary as the most important event in our time. When I consider today's assessment of Pius XII – not just by Hochhuth – I remember how fervently we listened to his every word during the war, the words of a man whom we honoured unconditionally as the Holy Father.

During the day, I had the opportunity to work in the library and do basic research for a number of articles on the history of the Cistercians' Menelogium. The crucial event during this retreat was an old priest's unique introduction to contemplative prayer, involving a very moving description of one's most personal difficulties. I was profoundly impressed by his statement: 'I have often suffered physical pain while saying this prayer'. I shared this instruction with a young fellow student of architecture who had accompanied me from Dublin. He had initially attracted my attention in our local parish church at home because of his exceptional composure.

Over the years I had been able to publish articles in most of the more important little magazines printed by the Jesuits, Dominicans, Carmelites, Franciscans and Passionists. My speciality had been specific studies of the wording of blessings in the *Rituale Romanum*, particularly those concerning the laity, such as blessings of tools, buildings, food, etc. I acquired a clear and suitable style for these readers through the inspiration of a woman who was working in an entirely different medium. Searching for private pupils in early 1940, I came across Erina Brady in a boarding house, who embraced me when I mentioned that I had seen and admired her teacher, the dancer Mary Wigman. Raised on the continent by her highly educated father, she was tall with a proud gait, silky black hair, and wide-open eyes. She heralded a new order, which had overcome both slavery and narrow-mindedness. Her love-hate relationship with Irish Catholicism (shared by James Joyce, Frank O'Connor and many others) found an outlet in the desire to overcome threadbare and repressive morality. She wanted to bring the art of dancing to young Irishmen and Irishwomen as a means of expressing themselves beyond the stiffness of traditional folk dancing and the paltry imitation of America. She failed. As soon as the war was over she moved back to the Continent. I wrote to tell her how sorry I was that she had gone, while we were still privileged to remain in Ireland. She never replied. This was a bad omen. Many years later at Zurich airport, where Irish people often meet amid arrival and departure of Irish planes, I heard that she had died alone in a clinic in Lausanne. She personified the saying that 'Whoever has art, had religion'. In memory of the clarity with which she was able to explain the significance of differences in the direction of movement I dedicated a small piece on the theme 'Space Movement in Liturgy' to her.

De Valera had vowed that he and his cabinet members would make the pilgrimage to Lough Derg, should Ireland come through the war unscathed. On this pilgrimage one leaves Dublin early in the morning on an empty stomach and arrives at the 'red sea' in the northwest of the country around midday. One is then brought over to the rocky island by boat, where one remains for two full days. Shoes and socks are taken off: the acts of penance involve pacing around the ancient stone rings and around the Church while reciting prescribed prayers. Once a day black tea and dry bread are available. The first night is spent awake and in prayer. During the summer months special daily trains bring pilgrims from all over the country. Some businesses close for three days to give the entire staff an opportunity to participate in the pilgrimage. As an old man De Valera fulfilled his promise. In Lough Derg one could meet university professors, civil servants, factory managers, office workers, students, farmers and people from the slums who had been given the price of the ticket by a benefactor. An old woman from a remote mountain village said to me: 'I've been coming for 40 years and have never got what I prayed for'. There is a most joyful atmosphere among those returning from this unique pilgrimage. An acquaintance made on this journey is supposed to secure a good marriage. On arriving in Dublin I heard a pretty girl tell her mother, who came to meet her, 'Uh, it was great gas'. This after 1500 Hail Marys.

On my return from the pilgrimage I wrote down my impressions. I went again the following year. When the sun is setting behind the mountains the pilgrims sit on the landing pier as the stillness of the lonely countryside settles over the crowd. Beside me sat two girls. In the midst of the silence one of them said: 'That's exactly what Hennig described'.

PEACE

A few days after the end of the war I received two letters from the University. The first one informed me that I had to pass an exam in mathematics in order to continue my studies in architecture, the second one, that I was no longer needed to teach German now that the 'emergency' was over. The *Standard* wrote to say that my contributions were no longer needed. From Maynooth came the news that my position had to be filled by a cleric. Although these bad tidings were nothing compared to the news of the horrors that reached us from the mainland, they drove me to the edge of despair. We had been blessed with a third child, and perhaps it was this fact that gave my wife strength to urge me not to lose courage.

I went to a small hotel in the mountains to spend a few days alone. One evening I visited a farmer's family of our acquaintance. Their small son was ill and still in bed. I sat down next to him and, to entertain him, moulded little long-legged men out of clay. His mother came in: 'Oh, how funny. Just like those people from the concentration camps'.

Among the hotel guests was a couple from the suburbs of Dublin. They told me that a position as a German teacher was available at the

Technical College and that they would recommend me, although I was a foreigner ... I got the job.

In the first weeks after our arrival I had lain awake night after night hearing the screams from the concentration camps. At the time, friends tried to quieten me, telling me that I saw things too gloomily, and frankly that it was no good tormenting myself. Now, when I hear everywhere that nobody knew anything, I ask myself how I knew about it. Every night during the war we said the liturgical prayer for the living and the dead with our children because we did not know whether our loved ones, no matter where they were living, 'were held back in the flesh by temporal life or whether eternal life had already received them, free of earthly bonds'. Now the news came quickly. It seemed as if we had passed the halfway point in our lives, for the list of the dead for whom we had to pray got longer than that of the living. Only within the circle of our immediate family were there miraculously no losses to be mourned. The great rescue campaign began. Victor Gollancz called for action. They asked us in Belfast for addresses of those in need. I was crushed by our own helplessness.

But even in Dublin I was faced with a standard by which to measure my own position. At a service in the pro-cathedral we were approached by an elderly woman. She had noticed that my wife was using a Latin-German missal. She used to be a governess in Bohemia. She had managed to flee home again by circuitous ways but had lost all of her savings. Now she was living in the cellar of a dilapidated house in a tiny room with space for a bed, a washstand and a chair. She did her cooking in used tins on a gas burner. Her government pension was barely enough to pay the rent.

But if anybody was a lady, she certainly was. She spoke cultivated English without affectation, she read only the best books, which she borrowed from friends, and she understood every problem and, above all, had compassion for all who were suffering. Every time we ran into her later on, we learned that she had just taken a drunkard to his home, had prevented an unmarried pregnant girl from killing herself, had persuaded a man to stay with his family or had comforted a child with a sweet. We often did not see her for weeks but when we met again, she knew everything that had happened to us and she had kept us in her prayers. One day the police called. Did we know Miss Smyth of No. 34 Gardiner Street? She had been found, and had been dead already for three days. On the table lay a letter addressed to her from us. Today we are probably the only ones who still remember her.

A few days after receiving my naturalization papers, I learned through an advertisement in the newspaper that the government agency for peat moss production was looking for a Records Officer who knew German and French. I didn't know what a Records Officer was. I went to the interview and was hired. My place of work, however, was a two-and-a-half-hour bus ride away from home. For three years I could only go home at weekends. From Monday to Friday I spent my evenings in the deserted offices located in barracks of Napoleon's time. I remember having to interrupt my typing of an essay on the tradition of St. Cataldus of Tarento because one of the rats that shared my room was altogether too boisterous. I lodged with a very old woman who was the pious town's gossip. I was alternately subjected to gossip and motherly care.

The abysmal dreariness of a small Irish town overwhelmed me. After evening devotions, people went to the cinema to watch the dregs of the American film industry, to dog races, or to the pub. My consolation was early morning Mass, for which my landlady woke me without fail, once she had noticed that I was 'attentive', as the saying went. The manager of the small lending library let me have a key and permitted me to work there until late in the evening. The library owned amazing things, for instance, an entire set of the journals of the Antiquarian Society, which I studied from A to Z in order to index all the localities, churches, works of art, etc, that were related to the saints. It was one of the many things that I have never been able to make use of.

Tired of being separated, we decided to look for a piece of land where we could build a little house near the place where I was working. I began negotiations with a woman but we didn't make much progress and there were, in fact, more important things to discuss. She asked me for advice about her daughter who had fallen in love during the war with a German interned in the military camp nearby. After his return to Germany, she had supported him with food packages from her own meagre supplies. Then came a letter saying that his mother insisted on breaking off the relationship because of the difference in religion. In

Ireland at that time the average marrying age for women was 35; the number of women who never married was larger than in any other country. The usual Irish story: the father had spent his life in pubs and on the racetrack and died early, leaving the entire responsibility on the mother's shoulders. Now she was left in her tiny cottage with two disappointed daughters. Having told me her story, she pointed to the picture of the Sacred Heart above the fireplace and said, 'Without Him I would not have survived'. When Marx's comment the opium of the people is properly quoted, it makes good sense; one could learn from the children of darkness, the lengths they will go to gain possession of precious goodness.

In my evening walks through the bogs, I rediscovered my interest in astronomy, kindled in my childhood days by a visit to the planetarium in Leipzig. At the Astronomical Society in Dublin, I found others who shared my interest in a thoughtful contemplation of the subject. I spoke of the basic experience of the tension between the realisation of the smallness of our earth, and the awareness of the dignity of man who is capable of perceiving this smallness. During the war the searchlights that we could see piercing the skies across the Irish Sea seemed like symbols of angels to me. I think the comparison would have soured had I been forced to experience for myself what those searchlights meant.

In the first years after the war I became especially conscious of being caught in the perspective that the circumstances of life had forced upon me. In connection with a book by the Dutchman Nico Rost, imprisoned in Dachau, I wrote a paper, 'Goethe in the Border Situation', in which I discussed Goethe's last essay on *Plastic Anatomy* having been stimulated by hearing about 'resurrection men', i.e. body snatchers, who worked for anatomists under the direction of an Irishman. Basically, the paper was concerned with investigating cultural values in border situations. However, I have to turn a deaf ear to those who say to me, 'How lucky you were to not have lived through the war'. And yet, I could never subscribe to the 'serves-them-right' attitude among the refugees, although only too understandable. Isolated as I was during the week, I felt as if my existence was concentrated in a single point, or better still like a very thin sound on the violin. The financial hopelessness was a mere symbol.

As the first sign of a friendship that had survived, Jaspers sent me his monumental work *On Truth*. Few readers will have studied it under circumstances as extreme as mine were in my barracks office at the smoky peat fire. In coming to grips with the greatest work of German post-war philosophy, I sensed that my mental life had not altogether atrophied. I had remained young by aspiring not for confirmation but for change.

All of my colleagues in the peat company were personalities. We were the experimental station and it was my job to find literature on the subject. Our director was an English convert and I was his godfather when he was confirmed. He had learned how to be a leader of men with the British Army in Burma. One could not help being moved by the struggle of our chemist, whose natural piety, though hidden under a very gruff shell, was still intact and occasionally succeeded in conquering his need to imbibe. In the first weeks I had to share lodgings with a little technical draftsman. On hearing him pray, I said he must have a good mother. He sighed 'Oh, dear Irish mothers, the damage they were capable of doing leaving their beloved sons to stumble along, timid, aimless and with no self-reliance'. The lucky ones, like our laboratory assistant, chose to join a spiritual community and he was to flourish on the mission.

The women workers usually possessed far more inner strength than their male colleagues. The high esteem in which women have been held since time immemorial stood in great contrast to the contempt for their psychophysical lives. The pubs provided the external framework for the lowest kind of purely masculine and therefore uninhibitedly vulgar social contact. Women were permitted to consume alcohol only in the dark entrances to the pubs. The disappointed ones among them set the tone with their cynical views on life. The women with whom we worked were able to retain their natural and supernatural qualities in part because we were a well-integrated and cheerful group. The knowledge that the burden of life would make them age early lent urgency to their desire to make the best of their brief years of bloom. A word of praise about their good taste in clothes, jewellery or hairstyle met with the rejoinder, 'One can see that you're a foreigner'. The rural, matter-of-fact attitude towards sex was difficult to reconcile with the Jansenism that was being preached from the pulpit. Ireland probably has fewer sex crimes than any other country in Europe.

Keyhole journalists, however, claim that this is only a false front, that all sorts of things happen behind closed doors. (It's an old story: already in the Middle Ages, Swiss goatherds were accused of sodomy by the Germans.) *The Tailor and Ansty,* a book considered obscene, fell victim to the strict censorship that prevailed, and promptly turned into a bestseller. At a club of enlightened Catholics in Dublin I attended one of the endless debates on censorship. In the end I decided to speak up. I began, 'I have had the misfortune of having lived for years in a country without censorship' (I was thinking of the horrible impressions made upon me by news stands when I was a child). 'Let's hear that again', somebody called out, 'did you say misfortune?' I advocated censorship within reason, perhaps without sufficient knowledge of bureaucratic red tape. After the meeting I was surrounded by people who had not dared to open their mouths, 'Of course we agree with you entirely'. Something similar occurred to me again recently when I wrote to a daily newspaper to complain about the insulting pornographic magazines which – apparently as a sign of intellectual freedom – cannot be suppressed .

As for the women with whom I worked over the years in Ireland, I must first praise the high level of their religious and even theological understanding. A fifteen-year-old flared up when one of our non-Catholic colleagues claimed that the Church taught that sins were remitted through indulgences. She did not simply rattle off the precise catechetical definition of indulgences; she complemented it with a first-rate explanation. This incident was the inspiration for my article on 'The Indulgence in the Eyes of a Layperson'. Today such an article would hardly stir any interest. It is true, we spent much of our employer's time chatting but, in retrospect, I believe that much of what we said was ultimately of benefit to the economy as well. I learned in those discussions not to shy away from broaching religious issues and I hardly ever met with any serious objections.

Examples of the endurance of suffering can only be acknowledged with silence, and Irish women have developed such skills to a high point. Rarely did I hear any complaints. The sick and the poor were considered worthy of respect. The measure of self-sacrifice in hopeless situations was probably still greater than elsewhere, especially among women. What must all those people I knew think today when faced with the breakdown of all the standards to which they sacrificed their happiness, birth control, mixed marriages, divorce – inconceivable human sacrifices. Were they a mistake? I believe I sensed all too often that the sufferers and those around them knew full well that a great deal more was at stake than the immediate issue. There are other values beyond what humanists call the greatest happiness of the earth's children.

C. S. Andrews was the Director of the Peat Company in my day and, to me, the best illustration of the new generation of enthusiastic but economically realistic Irish patriots. On my last visit, when I came to say good-bye, he asked me what had impressed me most about Ireland. Without a moment's hesitation I replied, 'The attitude towards death'. 'How strange', he answered. 'Yesterday my son said to me as we drove past the cemetery: Father, I don't think you will be all that sad once you have found rest over there', and to think that this man drove us almost to distraction with his energy. He ranted against the 'it-will-do' attitude that his compatriots had adopted under foreign domination. He enjoyed life, his struggle to counteract his country's lack of natural endowments, the prospect of a free people on free land, with human dignity, living in prosperity. But death was ever present. The knowledge of it even shone in the eyes of children. There was no clean, hygienic elimination of death from street life and certainly not from the family circle. The wake (known from the title of Joyce's last work, but also earlier from Goethe's poetic imitation of it in his *Irische Totenklage*) has been firmly ensconced in Irish life for centuries. 'I believe you are right', Andrews said, showing the highest approval an Irishman is willing to give.

And then things looked up as so often before. As soon as I told myself it can't go on like this anymore, a change would come from without. The need to fit my entire family life and library work into the week-ends, the long, lonely week-day evenings with their incommensurable activities, and having reached a conclusion in building up the records office were all reason enough for me to accept with delight the offer from the state-owned Electricity Supply Board situated in the heart of Dublin. In addition, it was a challenge for me to start from scratch again in a field where I lacked even the most basic skills.

It was hardest for me to take leave of the chief engineer. As a young man he had emigrated to America where he spent years working in tunnel construction. His health had suffered which lent the naturally reserved man a curious hardness. I once was talking to him about a talented older colleague. 'His most amazing quality', I said, 'is his modesty'. 'Modesty', replied the chief engineer, 'is all that counts'. He was not giving me a lesson, a maxim; instead it was the ultimate truth of a wise man. I saw him once again many years later. I told him how much these words of his had meant to me. He parried, laughingly, 'Well, didn't I learn quite a bit from you?'

Another man of wisdom, whom I met through my work in peat production, was Kotri Hangelaid, former director of the peat industry in Estonia. He had been a cadet under the Czar. In 1940 he managed to flee to Sweden with his wife and younger son. His older son disappeared in Siberia. Hangelaid was called to Ireland for a short time as an advisor. I was appointed as his interpreter and aide in his task of testing one of the gigantic bogs in County Mayo, the most poverty-stricken area in the country, for mechanical peat production. We often stood at a spot from which one could see nothing but bog as far as the eye could reach. Hangelaid, out of his deeply religious understanding of nature, drew my attention to marvellous features of flora and fauna. There were birds that faked an injured wing when one approached their defenceless brood, and then limped along in front of one's feet to lure one away. After only a few steps it was impossible to find the nest again. There were plants that sent their roots through the layer of peat deep down in the bed of loam. Symbols of life ...

Hangelaid was a product of the Protestant way of life, self-confident, with the pride of the nobility, hard on himself and others, honest and diligent. He set standards. He epitomized for me the national schism in the ecclesiastical sphere. He could not feel at home in the Anglican Church because of its political alignment with England. He was torn. His country had been one of the least anti-Semitic in the world, yet he could not rejoice in the victory of the Russians. He suffered from not being able to play his beloved organ. He was repelled by the proletarianism of the Catholic Church. He felt persecuted as a non-Catholic. Age and circumstances prevented him from looking behind the façade. I tried to explain to him how deeply the respect for things that were part of his life was mirrored in the prayers but he remained distant. He became annoyed when I took the conservative view in the discussion on Princess Margaret's plan to marry a divorced man. When he was no longer needed, he left, an embittered man. We saw him once more later, in his last place of refuge in Uchte, on the edge of the Oldenburg. He showed us a gold medal he had been awarded for playing the organ at the local church.

Our closer colleagues were aware of the disgrace of this man's dismissal. In Ireland, not only the rich man but also the successful one was considered a subject of ridicule rather than of admiration. The saying, 'But for the grace of God, there go I', was as common as 'Well, that's the way God made him'. When I started my job at the Electricity Board, the chief engineer there felt compelled to tell me, 'Here we have to make life as pleasant for each other as possible. Life is too short. Eventually we have to go anyway'. This was a lesson I had already learned years ago.

Shortly after I had begun to be on firm ground again, thanks to my position at the Electricity Board, an official who saw me working in his library everyday told me, 'My God, the life you have led in recent years would have broken many a better man than you'. He knew only the half of it. In my life of two occupations, my left hand never knew what my right hand was doing. In an academic paper on old-English martyrologies, I indicated in a footnote that a certain form of chronology in medieval calendars was based on the same reasoning as the calculation of electricity rates in peak hours and non-peak hours. On the other hand, how often have I quoted words from the 'Blessing for all things'? Out of happiness at being able to serve a cause through subordination (in the sense of Rilke) to the inherent laws of, for instance, a raw material.

The change that comes over the Irish as soon as they work in foreign countries later helped me to understand the Italian 'guest' labourers in Switzerland but although they have the additional language handicap, they are generally more robust by nature. Later, at the St. Patrick's Day get-togethers at the Irish embassy in Berne, I heard many complaints from girls employed on the continent as typists, nurses, domestics, or in the hotel trade because of difficulties due to the clash not only of their education, today decried as repressive, but also of their own deepest nature with the supposedly great outside world.

My day at the Electricity Board ended at 5 p.m. From then on I did not have to give my job another thought and could devote myself to my 'real' life, as Arthur Cox had called it. During the day I was able to see to it that the libraries had the books I needed ready for me in the evening. I began working for the radio especially on matters of ecclesiastical music. Numerous discussion groups invited me to participate. Years before I had gone to a club with the Grabisches, which was concerned with the promotion of women's rights, a somewhat antiquated undertaking since women have since attained the highest positions in business and government. A paper was read on Gertrud von Le Fort, a name completely unknown to most of those present. The first participant in the discussion said: 'Some of the poems that were recited were so bad, they could have been written by a man'. I had learned long ago that everything depends on playing up to a sense of humour. (Ernst Lewy, the great linguist, said: 'The only thing Irish take seriously is their jokes'.) But what followed was a gripping statement on the fate of the single woman, how she was put off with devotional exercises and her lack of opportunity for creative expression. My professional business work often brought me in contact with women. But in the discussion I was confronted with a situation that has time and again condemned me to silence. Women are even more disillusioned than coloured people or Jews, so much so that they cannot believe a man would seriously take up their cause. It is the insurmountability of the limits of human existence, which I later took as a starting point in expositions on the mutual relationships of angels (a largely neglected subject). Experience has robbed me of any missionary zeal. Nothing is left for me but description. Only rarely is it possible to break through the barrier for a moment.

The last time I accepted the invitation of a debating club I spoke about existentialism, which the Irish view as a kind of youthful mental hooliganism. In the discussion an old lady got up: 'The speaker has said that truth is based on veracity. But truth exists on its own and is independent of veracity, as desirable as the latter may be'. I sensed the depth of her uneasiness, of her dismay even, and felt like an arsonist.

In Ireland, the word 'existentialism' was mentioned for the first time – I am almost sure of it – in my lecture in June 1940 at Trinity College to the students' association that grandly called itself *metaphysical*. When Joseph Hone learned that I knew Jaspers personally and had read Heidegger, he arranged for me to meet his friend Arland Usher. Usher gave me the manuscript that was published later under the title *The Face of Ireland* – he had little appreciation of the intellectual life of Ireland. It was not up to me to tell this man, deeply rooted in Irish language and literature, that I am an outsider, considered his view neither comprehensive nor profound. Usher asked to borrow some of the books to which I had access, above all Jasper's *Geistige Situation (Intellectual Position)*. His essay 'Afterward to Existentialism' was published a few months later. It was a little too soon for it.

To Hone, the sensitive literary historian, public success had been denied. The nationalists rejected him as Anglo-Irish. The Modernists probably could not forget that Hone had been held responsible for the delay in publishing Joyce's *Dubliners*. The first page of his George Moore is not only a classical text of English Literature but also one of the greatest personal descriptions of the fate of the Anglo-Irish, best compared to that of the Baltic-Germans. He invited me to collaborate on a *Dictionary of Irish Writers*, planned by him and Lennox Robinson. I specialised in examining the contribution of Anglican clergymen to Irish intellectual life. The often-strange fates of these men illuminated the circumstances that had formed the characteristic Anglo-Irish frame of mind to which we still owe the most important Irish contributions to world literature. Lack of interest brought the venture to a standstill. We never got beyond the letter 'C'. Only one of my 50 articles appeared in print. I never learned what happened to the other 49.

Through Joseph Hone we met his cousin Evie. She was a convert and a student of Gris and Braque. Her stained glass art was finally beginning to be recognised by top connoisseurs even in ecclesiastical circles. She lived and worked in a few rooms of a country home near Dublin. Her character and the ambiance around her radiated a culture, which was an oasis for us in the midst of often depressing mediocrity. Death overcame her on her way to holy Mass. The cartoon of a window depicting the crucifixion is one of our most precious possessions.

Neither existentialism nor another -ism (not even nationalism) had any particular significance in Ireland. None of the traditional categories apply, from 'Middle Ages' and 'modern times' down to 'revolution' and 'democracy'. More important still is the irresistible urge of the Irishman to be contrary even to himself. Not only will he contradict his partner on principle, i.e. for argument's sake, he is also liable to change his mind in the midst of a discussion, justifying himself only with a casual remark, 'I suppose you're right'. The basic concept of the ism, possibly inflated into a 'movement', is discredited by the irony of almost hoary wisdom. My neighbour, a high government official, once spent an evening talking to a Bahai follower. The next morning he said to me, 'Those people are touching. Basically, they talk about things that are as old as those hills' – and he pointed to the granite mountains across the bay. It was as if my father had spoken.

In Ireland it is not even necessary to learn the difference between objective and existential thinking, because what foreigners consider as Celtic twilight is only a variation of it. The overwhelming garrulity of the Irish conceals more than it reveals. Ireland is the only country in Western Europe that became Christianised without a single martyr. The holy tidings encountered a uniquely congenial temperament here or, to put it differently, their adaptation to existing circumstances was unique. The state of mind, whose expression was the Irish liturgy – the main theme of my historical research – has survived. I am not certain whether I shouldn't use the pluperfect here. Should Ireland succeed in making the transition into the age of technology without losing its soul, it would do an immeasurable service to all of mankind. Some of my Irish friends justify this hope of mine.

Years ago when I began these notes, I had planned at this point to describe the different forms of public worship to give a survey of what I had encountered in Ireland. Most of this would probably be history today, but not yet far enough removed to be of interest. Across the distance of time and space I do not dare judge later developments, especially the tendency, noticeable in Ireland as well, to outstrip the Second Vatican Council on the left. Shortly after the beginning of the Council, I attended a conference in Basel at which Mario von Galli discussed what lay ahead. I took the liberty of saying that I had encountered a life of faith in Ireland that was inconceivable to the average continental European. Galli retorted: 'Well, at the Council, the Irish certainly aren't playing a particularly pleasant role'.

In the face of such judgements, I withdraw into my modest, very personal experiences. In Ireland, the Biblical word, except ye become as little children, is not a sentimental summons but a statement of fact that is common knowledge. When the dogma of the Assumption of the Virgin Mary was announced, my mother wrote to me saying this would unfortunately deepen the gulf between Protestant and Catholic Christians. I told her that we were all sitting at the radio on the morning of the promulgation, and the moment the dogma was announced, a candle placed in the window of every house was lit. I met a typist on her to work who said, 'Now we know again what man's vocation is'. My mother's reply that it was now easier for her to understand what it meant to us filled me with joy.

Our children were able to grow up in inner peace thanks largely to Dominican nuns where they attended school. Of course, the standards were not comparable to Central European or English schooling. The effect of a Catholic educational tradition, battered for centuries, still lingers on. One might consider it a waste of time that the children have to learn the totally useless Irish language as a main subject. But one cannot underestimate the importance of cultivating values that are for once based on something besides material usefulness. By learning a language that actually embodies a culture, my children were able to enjoy an education that is at best transmitted elsewhere by learning Greek. They learned Latin from me in private lessons: they know how poorly vernacular translations compare with the original liturgical prayers. Having witnessed, as both a teacher and a father, what it means for an entire school to be imbued with a humane spirit oriented toward godliness – not in an artificial boarding-school atmosphere but in the midst of community and family life, I can no longer listen to discussions on the so-called denominational school without getting impatient.

Like my colleagues at work, all the teachers my children had were also personalities. I learned that convent life does not lead to uniformity after spending fifteen years observing how the sisters, mothers and Mother Superior came and went, and how they reacted to the different phases and circumstances in the children's lives. The sisters taught the children the rosary by entrusting them each with a mystery. Our second daughter came home, radiant, 'I got the scourging'. But she learned the profound significance of this coincidence. We had spared our children, as far as it was defensible, the burden of the horror from which they had been saved by the grace of God. I had adopted the idea suggested by an English religious order of linking the Stations of the Cross, a beloved form of personal devotion in Ireland, with the remembrance of tortured peoples.

Our children were familiar with the prayers for intercession long before they were restored to the liturgy. The Pope's worldwide appeal to remember the victims of a catastrophic flood in Italy was heeded spontaneously and generously and, of course, with practical deeds as well. When I was praying with the children on night, the youngest – six years old at the time – suddenly piped up, 'Daddy, floods'. The most striking aspect of this religious upbringing was its cheerfulness. *Laetatus sum* ... the joy of abiding in the House of the Lord, where Jews and Christians are united, was the highest goal. It would never have occurred to us to call attendance at Sunday Mass or Easter confession a 'duty'.

The sisters who taught in the school our children attended were unusually sympathetic to our special situation, more so than many lay Catholics. The children were rehearsing for a Passion play. One of the lines read, 'They all loved the Saviour, only the Jews hated Him'. It was to be recited with a great display of revulsion. Spontaneously our little ten-year-old went to the Mother Superior, who apologised to the child and immediately had the text altered. Leaving church on the previous Sunday, we had been offered *Fiat*, the paper of an anti-Semitic organisation inspired by a religious order, which tastefully called itself *Maria Duce*. I had gone to the vendor and told him, 'Having lost a dozen people closest to me in the gas chambers, I find your appearance here an insult'.

These problems not only came to us. We also had to look for them ourselves. On my first visit to England after having been issued an Irish passport, I soon became acutely aware of what we had been spared in Ireland.

Notes

[1] After arriving in Ireland, Hennig changed his first name from Johannes to John.

[2] Letter from Erica Becker, Ardross, Western Australia, 4.12.2000 to G. Holfter.

[3] One of these, John Hennig, *Literatur und Existenz – Ausgewählte Aufsätze* (Heidelberg: C. Winter 1980) was compiled by him. Further collections include: John Hennig, *Goethes Europakunde*, Rodopi 1987 (with a foreword by Karl Pestalozzi and an introduction by John Hennig), John Hennig, *Goethe and the English Speaking World*, Bern/Frankfurt et al: Peter Lang 1988 (with a foreword by Hans Reiss); John Hennig, *Medieval Ireland, Saints and Martyrologies*, ed. by Michael Richter, Northampton: Variorum Reprints 1989; John Hennig, *Liturgie gestern und heute*, Vol. 1 & 2, n.p. 1989 (privately published, 1184 pages, with an introduction by Angelus Häussling 'John Hennigs Beitrag zur Liturgiewissenschaft' and the chapter on liturgy by John Hennig in the privately published autobiography *Die bleibende Statt*). See also the bibliography entitled 'Dr. phil. Dr. phil. h.c. John Hennig 1932-1970', compiled by Emanuel v. Severus OSB, *Archiv für Liturgiewissenschaft*, Bd. 13, 1971, pp. 141-171. This bibliography is invaluable to research on Hennig; it was updated by Angelus A. Häussling OSB in 1978, with a supplement on publications between 1971 and 1976, (*Archiv für Liturgiewissenschaft*, Vol. 19, 1978, pp. 98-105), and again in 1986, the year Hennig died, including an index of all topics covered (*Archiv für Liturgiewissenschaft*, Vol. 28, 2, 1986, pp. 235-245).

[4] Cf. Patrick O'Neill, *Ireland and Germany. A Study in Literary Relations*, New York: Peter Lang 1985; Joseph Leerssen, *Mere Irish & Fíor Ghael*. Amsterdam/Philadelphia: John Benjamins 1986; Timothy Jackson, Die getouften von über mer – Zum Irland-Bild im deutschen Mittelalter, in: Y. Shichiji (ed), *Orientalismus, Exotismus, koloniale Diskurse*, Vol. 7, Munich: Iudicium 1991, pp. 263-274; Doris Dohmen, *Das deutsche Irlandbild*, Amsterdam/Atlanta: Rodopi, 1994; Gisela Holfter, *Erlebnis Irland – Deutsche Reiseberichte im 20. Jahrhundert*, Trier: WVT 1996; Joachim Fischer, *Das Deutschlandbild der Iren 1890-1939*, Heidelberg: C. Winter 2000.

[5] Published by the family on his 76th birthday on 3. March 1987. The title refers to a passage from the Bible, Hebrews, 13,14 'For here we have no continuing city but we seek one to come'. For Hennig, the Church was a 'continuing city' ('Statt' in old German Bible versions) in the great turmoil of his life (Statt, 9). The two chapters contained in *Die bleibende Statt* about Ireland are reproduced in this book.

[6] "Children, don't waste anything!' How often did we hear that. All leftovers were used up, and the most unbelievable dishes were then concocted to satisfy the many hungry mouths. (...) The same applied to our clothes. For years our parents wore long since worn-out coats, hats (!) and shoes without caring about the opinion of their contemporaries, just to afford us the bare essentials growing up', Ernst Hennig, *Wir fünf Henniggeschwister und unsere Mutter*, p. 11 (19 pages, no year, typescript; we thank Wolfgang Hennig, for allowing us access to his collection).

[7] Ernst Hennig, *Unsere Eltern – Ein Lebensbild niedergeschrieben von Ernst 1978*, p. 12, no place of publication, no date, 42 pp. typescript, held by Wolfgang Hennig.

[8] Letter from Erica Becker, 4.12.2000.

[9] Letter from John Hennig to Karl Hennig, 19.2.1981, held by Wolfgang Hennig.

[10] His logbooks with descriptions of experiences, thoughts and many historical observations can be found in the Exile ArchiveFrankfurt, John Hennig papers.

[11] A list in the *Curriculum Vitae*, which is appended to his degree documents, gives exact information: Evangelical Religion Studies: Hoelscher, (Bonn), Stoltenburg (Berlin), Leipoldt, Alt (Leipzig), Philosophy: Rothacker, Landsberg (Bonn), Spranger (Berlin), Driesch, Litt, Wach (Leipzig), Pedagogy: Feldmann (Bonn), Spranger (Berlin), Boehm, Litt (Leipzig), Psychology: Graf v. Duerckheim (Leipzig), German: Walzel, Quint (Bonn), Hermann, Petersen, Alewyn (Berlin), Frings, Karg, Korff (Leipzig), English: Quint, Schirmer (Bonn), French: Menzerath, Curtius (Bonn), History: Levison, Braubach (Bonn), Oncken (Berlin), Berve, Brandenburg, Hellmann, Scholz, Stimming (Leipzig), History of Art: P. Clemen (Bonn), Waetzoldt, Woelfflin (Berlin), Beenken (Leipzig). University Archive Leipzig, Phil Fak Prom 1430. His relationship with Levison is also brought to the fore in the *Bleibende Statt*. Levison likewise later had to go into exile. In a private recollection Hennig wrote to his brother Karl 'Of all my teachers at University, Erich Rothacker, who unfortunately later became a Nazi, influenced me the most, Litt did not influence me at all, although he was my supervisor, and Wach hardly influenced me at all. The historian Hellmann was a great man, as was the Old Testament specialist Alt. I am thankful to Leipoldt and Witkowski (German Professor) for their understanding'. Letter from John Hennig to Karl Hennig, 19.2.1981, held by Wolfgang Hennig, Stolberg.

[12] Karl Hennig (1903-1992), Protestant theologian, studied Theology, Philosophy, German and History at Leipzig and Cologne, in addition to completing his degrees in Philosophy and Theology in 1929, he was awarded a Master of Sacred Theology during his time in Hartford/Connecticut, where in 1930/1931 he was an exchange theologian. After three years as a pastor and religion teacher in Leipzig he took up a position in Antwerp, and in 1938 he took on pastorship for the diocese of Eupen-Malmedy and St. Vith. In 1945 he had to leave Belgium, despite the exertions of Nicole Limbosch who was a friend of John Hennig's father-in-law Felix Meyer. From 1946-1968 he was pastor in Stolberg, Aachen. Cf. Matthias Wolfes, Karl Hennig, in: *Biographisch-Bibliographisches Kirchenlexikon*, Vol. XVII, Herzberg: Traugott Bautz 2000, pp. 637-638 (www.bautz.de/bbkl) and letters of Felix Meyer, 30.7, 12.8, 24.8, 26.8.1945 (Exile ArchiveFrankfurt). Cf. also Amelis von Mettenheim, *Felix Meyer 1875-1950 – Erfinder und Menschenretter*, Peter Lang: Frankfurt a.M. 1998, p. 114.

[13] Letter from Hennig to Karl Hennig, 19.2.1981, held by Wolfgang Hennig, Stolberg.

[14] Cf. Amelis von Mettenheim, *Felix Meyer 1875-1950 – Erfinder und Menschenretter*, Peter Lang 1998, pp 21ff. He developed, above all, the rotameter, which determined exactly the amount of flowing gases and liquids and their velocity, as well as the automated manufacture of ampoules and catheters (cf. ibid. pp. 25f).

[15] Joachim Wach (Chemnitz 1898 - Orselina 1955), German religion sociologist; 1929-1935 Professor for Religious Studies at the University of Leipzig, 1935 prematurely relieved of duties (his mother was born Mendelssohn-Bartholdi), went into exile in the USA, first at Brown University in Providence/Rhode Island and 1945/6 at the University of Chicago.

[16] Theodor Litt (Düsseldorf 1880 - Bonn 1962), German Philosopher and Educationalist; 1920-1937 and 1945-1947 Professor of Philosophy at the University of Leipzig; was prematurely relieved of duties in 1937.

[17] University Archive in Leipzig, Phil Fak Prom 1430 Johannes Hennig.

[18] Felix Krueger (Posen 1874 - Basel 1948), German philosopher and psychologist, founder of the 'Leipzig School' of Psychology; 1917-1938 Professor of Philosophy and Psychology at the University of Leipzig.

[19] 'I can largely agree to the nature of the I. evaluation. The candidate is especially gifted, very intellectually flexible and especially responsive to the latest ideas in philosophy and their many nuances. He read and understood a great deal of material'. University Archive in Leipzig, Phil Fak Prom Hennig 1430.

[20] Ibid.

[21] Hennig had written to Wach and told him why he no longer had an academic career in mind. This news spread fast through the University via Wach (Statt, 99).

[22] University Archive in Leipzig, Phil Fak Prom Hennig 1430.

[23] Hennig's own recollection of the circumstances of his conferral are unclear. In *Die bleibende Statt* he explains: 'I am sure that not one of the assessors read a line of my dissertation. It was a vote of Nazis against non-Nazis. My dissertation was accepted with a one vote majority' (Statt, 100). As against that he writes in his essay 'Some Thoughts on Examinations' (*Hibernia*, May 1949, p. 130): 'No less than three of the professors under whom I had made special studies, were thus liquidated. They were permitted though to finish the examination of candidates they had already taken on. In my thesis I had voiced some criticism at Rosenberg's theory of history, and one of the two referees refused to accept my thesis on political grounds. In accordance with the university rules, a thesis on which the referees failed to agree had to be submitted to the whole staff of that particular faculty or school. This happened very rarely, but, in my case, as this was a secret ballot it afforded an unexpected chance of expressing academic disapproval of the new masters. (...) The great vote, which of course was ridiculously in my favour, made the subsequent oral a mere farce'. *Hibernia*, May 1949, p. 13f.

[24] Letter from Erica Becker, 12.7.2001.

[25] '

Unsere Eltern' - Ein Lebensbild niedergeschrieben von Ernst (Hennig) 1978, p. 34f (Appendix with letters) Letter from Johanna Hennig 5.12.1935 to the three sons and daughter-in-law, held by Wolfgang Hennig, Stolberg.

[26] Ibid., p. 22.

[27] Cf. Amalis von Mettenheim, *Felix Meyer*, p. 31.

[28] In an essay Hennig remembers the house: '(...) it dated from the sixteenth century, with stucco ceilings and a lovely staircase (The love of books). He also used a picture of Bodenhof for his article 'Irish Footsteps in Aachen' with the caption: 'Bodenhof, one of the castles characteristic of the Eifel mountains on the main road from Eupen to Aachen', *Irish Library Bulletin*, April 1948, p. 65.

[29] Amalis von Mettenheim, *Felix Meyer 1875-1950*, pp. 38f.

[30] Karl Jaspers (Oldenburg 1883 - Basel 1969), Professor for Philosophy and Psychology in Heidelberg, 1937-1945 ban on teaching, 1948 went to Basel, with Heidegger one of the leading proponents of existence philosophy.

[31] The New Thinking and the New Belief. A study on Karl Jaspers' 'Vernunft und Existenz' in: *Zeitschrift für Theologie und Kirche*, N.F. 17, pp. 30-52.

[32] In *Die bleibende Statt* (p. 116) Hennig states that the visit took place one year after their first meeting in 1937, therefore, it took place in 1938. However, thanks to information from Dr Suzanne Kirkbright, who is working on a biography of Jaspers and has an insight into extant letters, one can now say with certainty that the visit took place in 1939.

[33] National Archives, Department of Foreign Affairs, 202/417 (Hennig).

[34] Military Archives, G2/0467 Dr. Johannes Hennig.

[35] Exile ArchiveFrankfurt, John Hennig papers. The diary is A5 format. The handwritten entries describing the first weeks in Dublin are relatively detailed and give information about his daily routine, people he met, etc. Many of the notes, jotted down, are hardly legible (we thank Monica Schefold for her assistance in trying to decipher her father's handwriting).

[36] See Dermot Keogh on Irish Refugee policy, especially regarding Jewish citizens, *Jews in Twentieth-Century Ireland – Refugees, Anti-Semitism and the Holocaust*, Cork: Cork University Press, 1998, especially pp. 115-194.

[37] Military Archives, G2/0467 Dr. Johannes Hennig. This letter, which was obviously checked first by censors, can be found in documents with the note 'Letter, scribbled, English and German, from Henning (sic) to wife (then in Belgium) posted Dublin 10.10.39'. The passages in German are translated but parts of it were obviously not understood by the translator e.g. Hennig's judgement of the 'boy-teachers' (tutors presumably) '2-3' against which the censor has placed a question mark (Hennig has obviously used the German marking system [1=A, 2=B, 3=C, 4=C/D, 5=D/F, 6=F] to express his view that the tutors were reasonably proficient). Two further pages in the letter which aren't quoted here contain information for

Claire as to how best to undertake the journey with all the luggage, as well discussing items such as registration and financial matters.

[38] As described in the chapter from *Die bleibende Statt* reprinted in this volume. Erwin Schrödinger (1887-1961) stood coincidentally in the same row called out by the Immigrations Officer in England. In 1938 he fled from Vienna to Rome, and wrote to Eamon de Valera (1882-1975) who was leader of the Irish Government and also Head of the League of Nations at the time. De Valera, a former mathematician before he turned totally to politics, offered him a position in the newly created Dublin Institute for Advanced Studies.

[39] Schoolboy in Germany, in *Irish Monthly*, September 1946, pp.384-392, 384 (also in G. Holfter, H. Rasche (ed), *Exil in Irland – John Hennigs Schriften zu deutsch-irischen Beziehungen*, Trier: WVT 2002).

[40] Cf. with Hennig's essay 'Irland und der Nationalsozialismus', *Schweizer Rundschau* 47, 1947 (also in G. Holfter, H. Rasche, *Exil in Irland*): 'Of the twenty colleagues I had at a school run by a religious order, there was only one who did not want to see a German victory. One of my colleagues confided: 'We are happy if the Germans sink as many English ships as possible'. My landlady said: 'We'll see to it that the British don't win the war'. A highly educated, active and respected Catholic man said: 'I pray every evening for Hitler's victory'. A member of the Holy Order said: 'If Hitler were not attacking the Church, he would be a great man'. A high ranking government official: 'Hitler is totally right; of course he is only putting Communists into the concentration camps'. A seventeen-year-old wrote in a German essay: 'The Jews are vermin, and Hitler is right to exterminate them' (three months later the young man joined the R.A.F.)'.

[41] Perhaps the stamps which Felix Meyer enclosed with his letters from Belgium helped Hennig gain the affection of his students at the beginning. Cf. Felix Meyer to Hennig, 1.2.1940, Exile Archive Frankfurt, Felix Meyer papers.

[42] Telephone call G. Holfter to Desmond Fennell, Rome, 13.7.2001.

[43] Telephone calls, emails and interviews with Sean Schütte, Des Reynolds and John Hyland, former pupils of Belvedere College, June/July 2001.

[44] Letter from 2.5.1940 John Hennig to Marguerite Meyer. Cf. also letter on 5.5.1940 to Margot Junod (Exile Archive Frankfurt, Felix Meyer papers).

[45] Cf. How I learnt English, in *Irish Rosary*, March-April 1945 (also in G. Holfter, H. Rasche, *Exil in Irland*).

[46] Cf. Military Archives, Hennig File.

[47] Cf. the reprinted extracted in this edition from *Die bleibende Statt*, where Hennig describes how it was made known to him how he 'of course' would not be paid during the holidays. One can assume that Hennig did not want to unduly burden his mother-in-law with information about the difficult financial situation of his family.

[48] Exile Archive Frankfurt, Felix Meyer papers, letter from John Hennig 2.5.1940 to Marguerite Meyer.

[49] 'Provided we have an affidavit, we can have our emigration visa for USA in a couple of months. I enclose a form, which you will gather that the matter is terribly involved. Most Americans refrain from giving the required details about their financial situation to third persons, quite apart from the risk. Even if, say Herman or Max would be prepared to give us their guarantee, which, indeed, would not be too dangerous for them, as I surely would find a job, I doubt whether they would like to give sufficient details to make the affidavit valid. As it would be a non-relative-affidavit this point is essential (...) As a matter of fact, economical possibilities in this poor countries (sic) become more and more restricted, while all people who go to US, find decent jobs'. [written in English in the original] John Hennig to Margot Junod, 6.9.1940, Exile Archive Frankfurt, Felix Meyer papers.

[50] Cf. Letter from Hennig to Felix Meyer, 16.2.1941, op cit

[51] Cf. Amalie von Mettenheim, Felix Meyer, p. 31.

[52] Letter from Felix Meyer to John Hennig, 13.2.1941, Exile Archive Frankfurt, Felix Meyer papers.

[53] Card from John Hennig to Karl Hennig, 5.5.1940, op cit

[54] 'I do hope that I can arrange any kind of holidays for Claire. Although we have a very nice maid from 10-6, Claire has always to bother about the children and they are a hard strain. Sometimes Mrs. Hopf's daughter helps Claire with the kids but she is very unexperienced'. [written in English in the original] Letter from John Hennig to Margot Junod, 29.7.1940, Military Archives, Dublin, Hennig File G2/0467.

[55] Cf. with the letters from Felix Meyer to Ireland from 22.1.1945 ('Terrible, these family discordances in money matters! Luckily you are not like most families, on the contrary, you are the opposite'.) and 16.6.1945 ('Rereading your husbands letter I find, that he writes a very good English and I hope, I shall be able to hear him tomorrow on the wireless, but he made one great mistake, when he wrote about money which I had entrusted to you or to him. There has never been a question of enthrusting. Everything what was sent to you, is your and John's property and there has never been a question of paying back. Please dispose of everything you have left from such assets. Never there will come a moment when Mutti nor I will claim a farthing from such money'.) In January/February 1940 Felix Meyer implored his daughter and son-in-law to buy a further bed (Letters 24.1.; 1.2. and 10.2.) and after Gabrieles illness, he wrote forcibly: „(...) this is the moment for spending the extra shilling' (Easter Sunday 1940), [letter 16.6.1945 and Easter Sunday 1940 both written in English in the original] Exile Archive Frankfurt, Felix Meyer papers.

[56] Ludwig Bieler (1906-1981) was a Professor at University College Dublin for Middle Latin and Palaeography. His research topics included the lives of the Saints (especially the life of St. Patrick).

[57] Hans Sachs (1877-1945), Director of the Serology Institute in Heidelberg; the 'first German Serologist', according to Dean Richard Siebeck in 1933. 1935 he was forced to retire due to his Jewish background and emigrate in the following year. The Institute was closed.

[58] Letter from Hennig to Margot Junod, 29.7.1940, Military Archives, Hennig File.

[59] Ernst Hennig, Our Parents, p. 18.

[60] Peter Harbison remembered a violin which hung from the door (Interview 19.1.2001) and Thelma Sheehan, who was at school with Hennig's daughters, mention another friend who at roughly 6 years of age, went to a small party at the Hennigs. Hennig played something for the children on the violin and let them all try the instrument once (interview with Noel and Thelma Sheehan, 9.2.2001).

[61] John Hennig to Margot Junod 29.7.1940, Military Archives, Hennig File.

[62] Weekly Miscellaneous Report , D.M.D. – Week ended 29th April 1940, Military Archives, Hennig File.

[63] Weekly Miscellaneous Report , D.M.D. – Week ended 6th May 1940, Military Archives, Hennig File.

[64] '[...] I beg to report that above named Alien reported at Howth Garda Station on 13th July 1940, his intention of proceeding on a holiday tour to Connemara, County Galway of 14 days duration on 14th July 1940. He stated that he would be accompanied by the following persons: (1) Sydney Gibson, 'Rockford', Temple Rd, Rathgar, (2) Harry Nelson, 16 Royal Terrace, Fairview Dublin (3) James Guttrie, 11 Clareville Rd, Rathgar, Dublin and (4) Leslie Horton, 10 Furrypark Rd, Raheny, Co. Dublin. [Names underlined in red]. The party will travel in a Terraplane Motor Car No-Z. A. 8843 from Dublin to Fermoy, Co. Cork, where they will collect a living Caravan and then proceed direct to Connemara, County Galway. HENNIG is not actually suspect at present but it would be of interest to know whether he or his associates make suspicious contacts in Galway West Division during their holiday there. The Ard Cheannphort Galway has been informed of the contents of this report for guidance in the matter if supervision. A copy of this report is being furnished to Leas Coimisineir D.M.D. to ascertain if any of the present associates of HENNIG have come under notice of Special Branch in any subversive or suspected activities. I am calling for report regarding Leslie HORTON the only associate of HENNIG who resides in this division. ARD Cheannphort W.P. Quinn (Military Archives, Hennig File, 16.7.1940). On 29.7.1940 a more detailed report is given on the informant.

[65] Military Archives, Hennig File. M.J. Wymes, Sair 7845.

[66] Military Archives, Hennig File. A similar notice can be found in the archives dated 10.3.41: 'Would you please get the particulars of this man? His date of arrival is given as 6/10/39. can this be correct? When did his wife arrive? I have an idea he was here before then. If 6.10.39 be correct, how did he get here? As he then could hardly have contacted Clissmann, the story of his getting Cls pupils can hardly be

likely'. Helmut Clissmann had been the DAAD representative in Ireland and had travelled to Germany before the outbreak of the war. He came under the suspicion of the authorities for carrying out spy activities, cf. Horst Dickel, *Die deutsche Außenpolitik und die irische Frage von 1932-1944*, Wiesbaden: Steiner 1983, p. 77. There is a similar notice from 11 July 1940, G2 mentioned Clissmanns pupil to P. Carrol, Chief Supt. Garda Siochana Headquarters, Kilmainham – and more exact information was requested.

[67] For more information on censorship in Ireland during the war years, see Donal Ó Drisceoil, *Censorship in Ireland 1939-1945*, Cork: Cork University Press 1996.

[68] This file concerns Kurt Werner, another German in Ireland, who had written to Swiss journals and had offered them his reports about Ireland. Werner received a publications ban and was forbidden from conducting any form of correspondence with journals (Military Archives, OSS 7/31 – Controllers' office / Information regarding aliens)

[69] Military Archives, OSS 7/31 - Controllers office / Information regarding aliens. Thomas J. Coyne was 'Controller of Censorship' since September 1941, cf. Dermot Keogh, Twentieth Century Ireland, Dublin 1984, p. 125. A copy of the letter (without a signature) with smaller variations can be found in the files; there it is termed „anti-German propaganda' rather than 'anti-Axis propaganda'.

[70] Military Archives, OSS 7/31, Duff to Coyne, 11.6.1942

[71] Letter to J.E. Duff on 30. June 1942 (without a signature, but most probably from T. Coyne): 'In reply to your letter of yesterday's date (69/80/477) we have no objection to Dr. Hennig's continuing to contribute articles on liturgical subjects to the English Catholic Press. I have no doubt that he knows very well the type of stuff we don't want him to write and that the warning he has received will be efficacious'. Military Archives, OSS 7/31.

[72] Letter from John Hennig, 17.8.1942 to the Dept of Justice, Military Archives, OSS7/31. Unfortunately it was not possible to find out which article it concerned.

[73] J.E. Duff to T. Coyne 27. August 1942, Military Archives, OSS 7/31.

[74] Joseph Walsh, (1886-1956) Secretary of the Department of Foreign Affairs, after the war became ambassador to thr Holy See.

[75] Information from the Personnel Department of the National University of Ireland Maynooth, 19.9.2001. Father Patrick Twohig, former student of the seminary, still remembers well meeting Hennig 4.2.2001), albeit in a puzzling context: he is supposed to have shown his students the weals on his back which he received in a concentration camp (cf. J. Fischer, *Das Deutschlandbild der Iren*, p. 491). No trace of this can be found either in Hennig's own recollections (cf. Statt, 153), or in his daughter's recollections.

[76] Thelma Sheehan, who was at school with the oldest Hennig daughter, still remembers the event well, because Hennig, who became lonely while Claire was in

hospital, went to collect his daughters from school and brought them back 1-2 hours later – much to the shock of the prioress. Interview with Thelma Sheehan 9.2.2001.
[77] Interview with Prof. John Harbison, 9.2.2001.
[78] In May 1941 bombs were dropped (probably in error) on North Strand in Dublin and more than 30 people died. The German government made an official apology and paid compensation to the sum of £327,000 in 1958. Cf. Dermot Keogh, *Twentieth Century Ireland*, Dublin: Gill & Macmillan 1994, p. 123.
[79] Robert Collis (1900-1975), Pediatrician and Author, founded the Cerebral Palsy Ireland Society in 1948.
[80] 'You both once asked our opinion about whether or not you should adopt a child. May I say to you, that I would be very against it. (...) I hope you don't carry out such folly just to oblige your doctor. Something like this can have worse consequences than a marriage entered into without due thought'. Letter on 6.10.1945 from Felix Meyer to John and Claire Hennig, Exile Archive Frankfurt, Felix Meyer papers.
[81] Military Archives, Hennig File.
[82] Cf. *Irish Independent*, 2.1.1946.
[83] Exile Archive Frankfurt, Felix Meyer papers, letter from Felix Meyer to Margot Junod, 11.7.1946.
[84] Frank Gallagher (1898-1962), first editor of the *Irish Press* founded by De Valera. Director of the Government Information Bureau 1939-48 and again from 1951-54. He then worked at the National Library in Dublin. His daughter Ann still clearly remembers Hennig's frequent visits to Frank Gallagher and the unusual parties at the Hennig's with milk and 'Madeira biscuits' (presumably spicy almond biscuits). The friendship was not only confined to Hennig and Frank Gallagher and there was also close contact between the children. Daughter Ann was a school-friend of both Hennig's eldest daughters. Interview with Ann Gallagher and Paula O'Kelly, 9.2.2001.
[85] Card from John Hennig to Karl Hennig, 6.12.1946, held by Wolfgang Hennig.
[86] Letter from Felix Meyer to Margot, 11.7.1946, Exile Archive Frankfurt, Felix Meyer papers.
[87] Letter from Erica, Ardross, Western Australia, 4.12.2000.
[88] Letter from Hennig to Felix Meyer, 5.11.48, Exile Archive Frankfurt, Felix Meyer papers.
[89] Letter from Hennig to Felix Meyer, 10.8.1949, *op cit*
[90] John Cooke, *Bord na Móna Research Centre*. Bord na Mona, Kildare 1991, p. 67.
[91] C.S. Andrews, *Man of No Property - An Autobiography*, Cork, Mercier 1982, p. 196.
[92] *Architectural Design*, Vol 17, July 1947, pp. 195f.
[93] Dr. Peter Harbison referred to his impish humour and also told of various episodes and stories which confirm this (probably primarily from the period after the war years), Interview with P. Harbison, 19.1.2001. Prof. Hans Reiss also remembers Hennig's humour, email 27.9.2000.

[94] Exile Archive Frankfurt, Felix Meyer papers, letter from Felix Meyer to John & Claire Hennig, 6.1.1947. 'Little monk' was Hennig's second daughter Monica, who at the time of the letter was just nine years old.

[95] Exile Archive Frankfurt, Felix Meyer papers, letter to John Hennig (Meyer is refererring to an incident in Dublin when Hennig rescued some potatoes which had already been thrown away), 20.2.1949.

[96] Hans Reiss (born 1922) came to Dublin as a young exile to complete his school education. He studied in TCD and became assistant teacher of German there, a job for which Hennig had also applied, email Hans Reiss 27.9.2000.

[97] E.g. Goethe's friendship with Anthony O'Hara, *MLR* 1944, Jean Paul in Ireland, *MLR* 1945, The Brothers Grimm and T. Crofton Crocker, *MLR* 1946. See Royal Irish Academy 'Certificate of Candidate, John Hennig', signed 19 January, on 27 January 1947 it was read out to the Academy.

[98] The protocol book of the Royal Irish Academy contains the following entry from 27.1.1947: 'The Secretary read the certificates of the following candidates for membership'. Among the eight names are those of Ludwig Bieler and John Hennig.

[99] Felix Meyer to Claire and John Hennig, 29.5.1949, Exile Archive Frankfurt, Felix Meyer papers.

[100] Letter from Felix Meyer to Hennig, 27.2.1949, *op cit*.

[101] Letter from Hennig to Felix Meyer, 9.12.1948, *op cit*

[102] Email Hans Reiss, 27.9.2000.

[103] Hans Saner, philosopher, Karl Jaspers' last assistant and editor of his works.

[104] Letter from Hans Saner, 6.8.2001.

[105] Letter from Karl Pestalozzi to John Hennig, 2.8. 1981, held by Monica Schefold.

[106] He dedicated his talk which took place on 3 June (which 'in contrast to the certainly very ideological talks of the other participants' was positively received) to his brother Karl, who one day later celebrated his 79th birthday. Cf. Letter from John Hennig to Karl 23. April 1982, held by Wolfgang Hennig, Stolberg.

[107] Letter from John Hennig to Karl Hennig, 19.2.1981, held by Wolfgang Hennig.

[108] Letter from Monica Schefold, 17.8.2001.

[109] John Hennig to Karl Hennig, 19.2.1981, held by Wolfgang Hennig, Stolberg.

[110] '[...] have now more or less come to terms with it all, out of gratitude that I am still alive and am indeed surrounded by so much love', Letter from John Hennig to Karl Hennig, 12.11.1980, held by Wolfgang Hennig.